Exploring
iPad Pro

iPadOS Edition

Kevin Wilson

www.elluminetpress.com

Exploring iPad Pro: iPadOS Edition

Publisher: Elluminet Press
Director: Kevin Wilson
Lead Editor: Steven Ashmore
Technical Reviewer: Mike Taylor, Robert Ashcroft
Copy Editors: Joanne Taylor, James Marsh
Proof Reader: Steven Ashmore
Indexer: James Marsh
Cover Designer: Kevin Wilson

eBook versions and licenses are also available for most titles. Any source code or other supplementary materials referenced by the author in this text is available to readers at

www.elluminetpress.com/resources

For detailed information about how to locate your book's resources, go to

www.elluminetpress.com/resources

Table of Contents

About the Author

With over 15 years' experience in the computer industry, Kevin Wilson has made a career out of technology and showing others how to use it. After earning a master's degree in computer science, software engineering, and multimedia systems, Kevin has held various positions in the IT industry including graphic & web design, building & managing corporate networks, training, and IT support.

He currently serves as Elluminet Press Ltd's senior writer and director, he periodically teaches computer science at college in South Africa and serves as an IT trainer in England. His books have become a valuable resource among the students in England, South Africa and our partners in the United States.

Kevin's motto is clear: "If you can't explain something simply, then you haven't understood it well enough." To that end, he has created the Exploring Technology Series, in which he breaks down complex technological subjects into smaller, easy-to-follow steps that students and ordinary computer users can put into practice.

Acknowledgements

Thanks to all the staff at Luminescent Media & Elluminet Press for their passion, dedication and hard work in the preparation and production of this book.

To all my friends and family for their continued support and encouragement in all my writing projects.

To all my colleagues, students and testers who took the time to test procedures and offer feedback on the book

Finally thanks to you the reader for choosing this book. I hope it helps you to use your iPad Pro with greater understanding.

Have fun!

iPads

As iPads have continued to develop and evolve, they have received more and more features not available on iPhones. Because of this, iPads now have their own operating system called iPadOS.

So what's an Operating System? An Operating System is a program that manages the device's hardware resources such as memory, processor and storage. The Operating System also provides a platform for you to run apps such as web browsers, maps, email, photos, games and so on.

The iPadOS user interface is a touch screen, meaning you can directly manipulate sliders, switches, buttons and icons on screen using your finger.

iPadOS has a main screen called the home screen containing icons that represent apps. You can download countless apps from the App Store - you'll find an app for almost anything you can think of.

Security has improved on these devices, you can unlock just with a finger print - no need to keep remembering a PIN.

Finally there's Siri, the voice activated personal assistant that uses natural language AI to interpret voice commands you speak out loud. You can ask Siri to send messages, dial a number, as well as search the web, and answer certain questions.

What's New?

The home screen has a few changes. The icons are now smaller, and in horizontal mode, down the left hand side you'll see your clock with app widgets for weather, calendar, siri suggestions, maps, and screen time.

Also introduced in iPadOS is dark mode. This reduces the amount of white on the screen making it easier on the eyes.

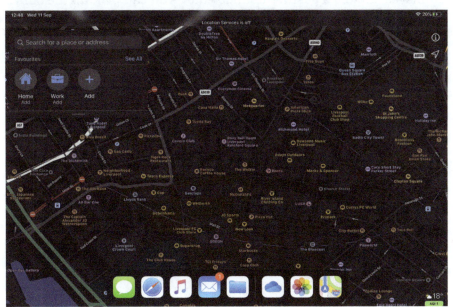

Chapter 1: iPads

iPadOS introduces a new feature called Sidecar that allows you to use your iPad as a second screen on a Mac running macOS Catalina. Useful for marking up documents, drawing and graphic design.

There are some new touch gestures you can use to copy & paste text or images, as well a gesture to undo edits. You can pick up the cursor and drag it precisely where you want it, or select a block of text by dragging your finger over it. You can also select a word with a double tap, a sentence with three taps, or a whole paragraph with four taps.

There is a floating on-screen keyboard you can position wherever you want, to make typing easier, as well as keyboard short-cuts should you want to add a physical keyboard.

Font management has been added to the iPad which allows you to install additional fonts from the App store should you need them for any work you are doing.

There are also improvements to multi-tasking features such as slide over and split view.

The photos app has had a few improvements including new tools to adjust and enhance photos, as well as a 'curated view' of your best shots. You can also apply effects and enhancements to video clips you have taken.

The files app on the iPad has been redesigned giving you a more detailed view of your files.

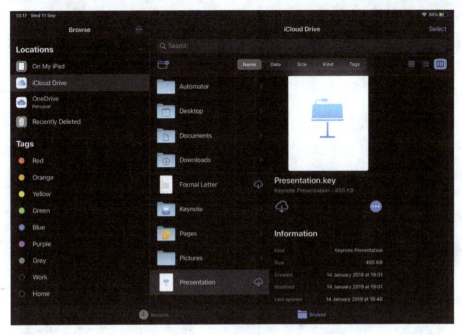

You can also connect to servers and plug in external drives such as flash drives and external hard disc drives.

Safari has a new download folder allowing you to view recent downloads and access them from the Files App.

Also introduced in iPadOS is Apple Arcade where you can play all sorts of new games.

Chapter 2

Setting up Your iPad

If you've just bought your new iPad and taken it out the box, the process to set it up to use for the first time is very simple. You don't even have to connect it to your computer.

At the time of writing, the new iPad Pros come in two sizes: 11" or 12.9" with liquid retina screen a silver or grey finish. There are four data storage sizes: 64GB, 256GB, 512GB & 1TB.

4 speaker audio and a 12 Mega pixel camera with 4K video recording

You can attach Apple smart keyboards and external bluetooth keyboards, useful if you use your iPad to do your work

Uses USB-C port for charging and external devices but has no 3.5mm headphone jack

Latest models only work with the second generation Apple Pencil.

In this section we'll take a look at setting up your iPad. Take a look at the video resources

www.elluminetpress.com/using-ipad-pro

Insert your SIM

Make sure your device is off before doing this. If your iPad has a SIM card or you're using an iPhone, you'll need to insert your SIM card from your network provider.

Push the end of a paper clip into the release hole on the side of your device. Pull out the little tray and insert your SIM.

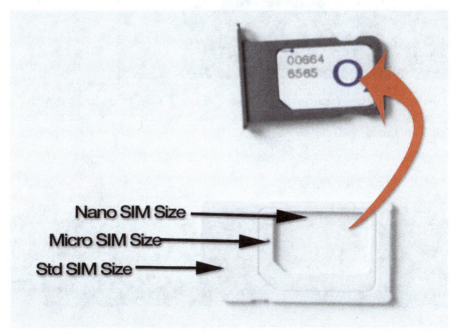

Chapter 2: Setting up Your iPad

Slide the little tray back into your device, until it fits firmly into place against the side.

You're now ready to power on your iPad. To do this, hold down the power button located on the top of your device, until you see the Apple logo on the screen.

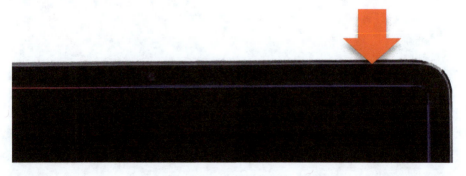

Give your iPad a few seconds to start up.

Power Up & Power Down

Once your iPad battery is fully charged, press and hold the power button for a couple of seconds until you see the apple logo.

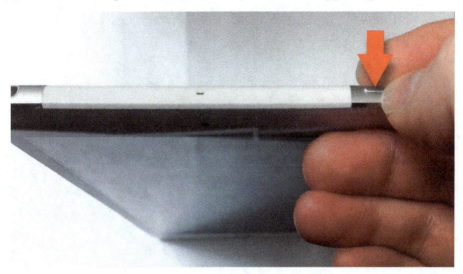

To completely shutdown your iPad, press and hold down on the top button and either the volume up button until a slider appears.

Slide your finger across the on-screen slider to confirm.

Upgrading your iPad to iPadOS

Make sure your iPad is plugged into a power outlet, and you are connected to your WiFi.

Once you have done that, go to the settings app, tap 'General', then select 'Software Update'.

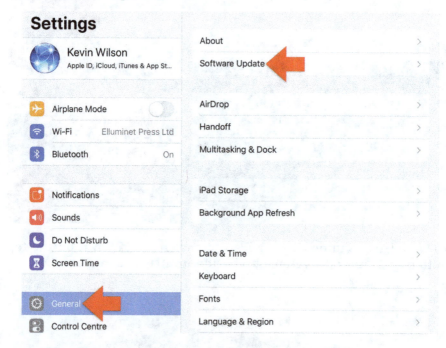

Tap 'Download and Install' on the available update.

To update now, tap 'download and install'. Enter your passcode when prompted. Your iPad will restart and the update will install. This might take a while.

Initial Setup

To use iPad, you need an internet connection and your Apple ID. Apple has introduced an automated setup feature that allows you to transfer settings from another device, such as an iPhone. Both devices must be running iOS 11, iOS 12, or iPadOS/iOS 13. If you don't have this, you can still set up your iPad manually. First lets take a look at the auto setup feature.

Auto Setup

Turn on your iPad. On the welcome screen, slide your finger across the screen, or press the home button to start.

Select your language and country/region.

Chapter 2: Setting up Your iPad

When you land on this screen, place your old iPad or iPhone next to your new iPad.

Unlock your old iPad or iPhone. You'll get a prompt on your old device, tap 'continue'.

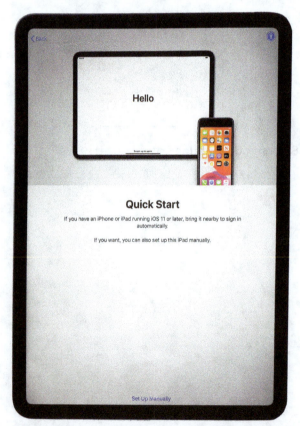

Now, you'll see a strange looking pattern appear on your new iPad's screen. Holding your old iPhone/iPad, position the pattern in the circle on your old device as shown below.

Keep your old iPad/iPhone next to your new one until the setup is complete.

Enter the passcode from your old iPad/iPhone, into your new iPad.

Set up Touch ID, sign in with your Apple ID when prompted.

Tap 'continue' on the 'go home' screen, 'quick access to the dock' screen, 'switch between apps' screen, and the 'quickly access controls' screen.

Manual Setup

Turn on your iPad, then from the welcome screen, swipe your finger across the bottom of the screen, or press the home button.

Select your language and country/region.

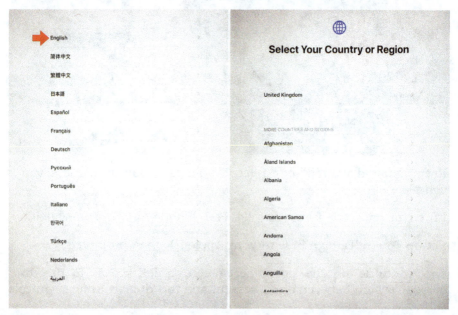

Select 'set up manually' on the bottom of the screen.

Select your WiFi network and enter your WiFi password when prompted.

Tap 'continue' on the data privacy screen.

Tap 'continue' to set up Touch ID.

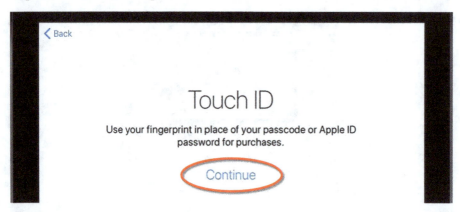

Now you need to scan your finger print. Scan the finger you are most likely to use to press the home button with. In most cases this is your thumb, so it makes sense to scan this finger. Follow the instructions on the screen.

You'll need to scan your finger a few times, so the system can account for different variations as you wont always put your thumb on the home button in exactly the same position every time. Do what it says on the screen. When you're done, tap 'next' on the top right.

Check out the Touch ID demo in the 'using iPad' section of the video resources on how to scan your fingerprint. Scan the code with your iPad or go to the following website.

www.elluminetpress.com/using-iPad-pro

Enter a 6 digit passcode. This code is used to unlock your iPad if Touch ID isn't available.

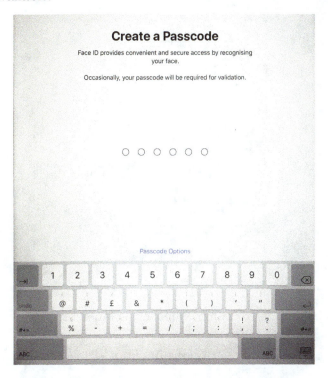

Tap 'restore from iCloud backup'. This will ensure all your settings, messages, contacts, apps, photos, music, and email are restored.

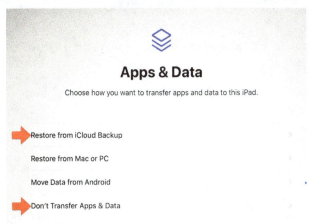

If you are setting up from scratch or are a new user, tap 'don't transfer apps & data'.

Chapter 2: Setting up Your iPad

Sign in with your Apple ID email address and password. Tap 'next' on the top right..

Choose a backup if prompted. Choose the latest one on the list.

Tap 'enable location services'. This allows your iPad to work out your physical location so you can get local information, weather, and map directions.

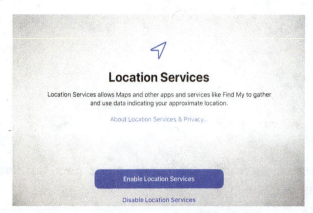

Tap 'continue' to set up Apple Pay. Follow the prompts to add your credit/debit cards.

Tap 'continue' to set up Siri. Follow the prompts on screen.

Tap 'don't share' on iPad Analytics.

Chapter 2: Setting up Your iPad

Tap 'continue' on the 'true tone display' screen.

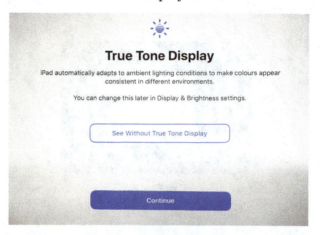

Select light or dark mode. Dark mode is much easier on the eyes and is good for low light and night time usage.

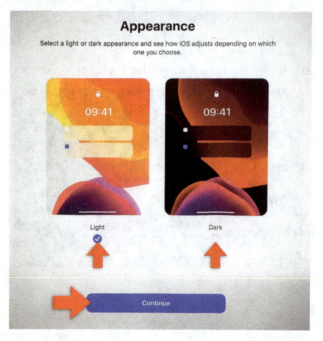

Tap 'continue' on the 'restore completed' screen if prompted.

Tap 'continue' on the 'keep your iPad up to date' screen

Tap 'continue' on the 'go home' screen, 'quick access to the dock' screen, 'switch between apps' screen, and the 'quickly access controls' screen.

Once you're completed the initial setup, you'll land on the home screen. See "Getting Around Your iPad" on page 58

Along the top of the home screen there is a status bar that displays current networks (cellular or WiFi), current time, services such as bluetooth and battery life.

In the centre of the screen are icons representing apps that are currently installed on iPad. Some are installed already but many can be downloaded from the app store.

Along the bottom of the screen is the Dock. The Dock is split into two sections. On the left hand side you'll see commonly used apps: messages, web browsing, email, music, and files. You can drag and drop icons onto this part of the dock from your home screen. On the right hand side of the dock, you'll see your most recently opened apps.

Chapter 2: Setting up Your iPad

This diagram shows the rear. You can see volume controls and SIM card tray on the left of the diagram. On the back you'll see your camera, the headphone jack along the top and the dock connector along the bottom.

Charging your iPad's Battery

You can plug your iPad directly into the charger to charge the battery, without having to go through a computer.

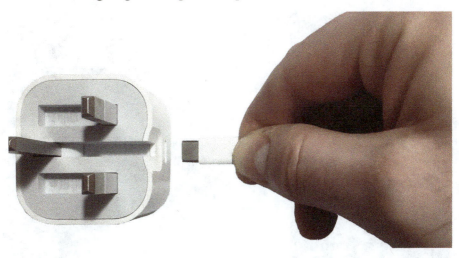

Plug the other end of the lightning cable into the port on the bottom of your iPad.

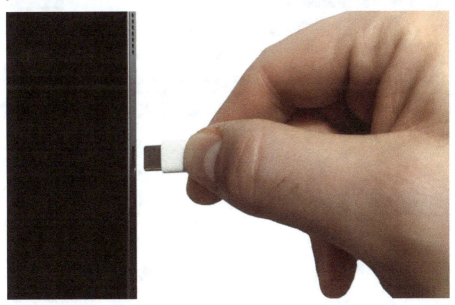

Your battery will take a few hours to charge. Best practice is not to let your battery deplete completely, charge it up when you still have about 20% charge left.

Connecting your iPad to a Mac/PC

Your iPad lightning cable connects to the port on the bottom of your iPad.

The other end of the cable can be plugged into a PC or Mac to allow you to load on music, photos, apps etc.

Using iTunes

To access iPad from your computer you will need to have iTunes installed. If you are using a Mac, iTunes is now called the Music App and will already be installed.

Tap the Music App icon on your dock or on Launch Pad

If you are on a PC then you will need to download iTunes from the Microsoft Store. You'll find the Microsoft Store on your start menu.

Type 'itunes' into the search field on the top right, then select 'iTunes' from the drop down menu.

Click 'install'.

You'll find the iTunes app on your start menu.

Chapter 2: Setting up Your iPad

Select the 'account' menu, click 'sign in...', then enter your Apple ID and password. Click 'sign in'.

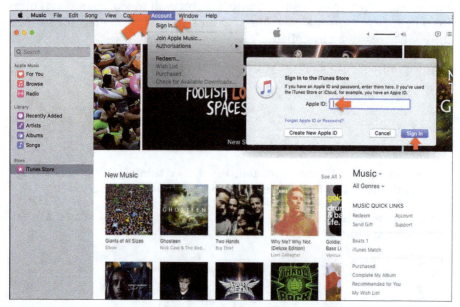

Sync your iPad/iPhone with your Mac

Plug your iPad into your Mac. Tap 'trust' on your iPad/iPhone if prompted. Open the finder app. Your iPad/iPhone will appear under 'devices' on the left hand panel. Click on your device.

If this is the first time you have connected your device to your mac, click 'get started'.

Here you can manage your iPad. Select 'general' for general settings, click 'music', 'films', 'tv programs', 'podcasts', 'audio books', and 'books' tabs to set auto sync between your mac to device,

From the 'general' tab, you can check for updates, or restore iPad if you're having problems. You can also back up your iPad to your computer or restore your iPad from a backup.

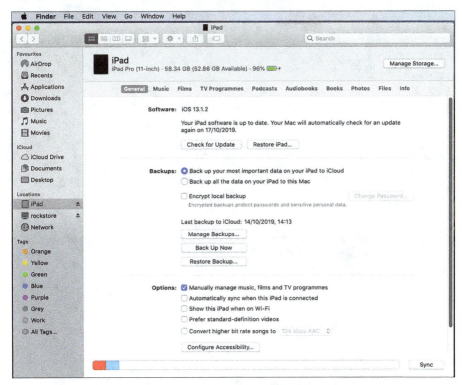

In the 'options' section further down the page, you can 'manually manage your music'. This allows you to drag and drop the music you want on your iPad from your mac. This is better if you prefer to choose what you to sync rather than syncing your whole music library on your mac.

Along the bottom, you'll see a data bar. This shows you how much space has been used on your device.

Restore iPad

You can restore your device to its factory settings if you have problems with it. Turn on your device and connect it to your mac. Open your finder app and select the device under the 'locations' section on the left hand panel.

On 'general' settings, click 'Restore iPad'. *If you have downloaded a restore image (IPSW), hold the option key and click 'restore' then select the image file.*

Click 'back up'.

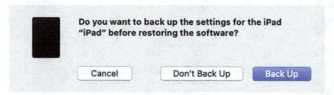

Click 'restore and update'

This will wipe your data, apps, music and settings, so you'll need to restore from a previous backup if you do this.

Connecting to the Internet

With an iPad, you can connect to the internet two ways: one is using WiFi and the other is using a cellular connection if you've inserted a SIM card. In this section, we'll take a look at connecting using WiFi

WiFi

WiFi is often faster than cellular data networks, but may not be available in some locations.

To locate nearby WiFi networks, tap 'settings' on your home screen.

Tap WiFi, then tap the name of the network you want to join

Enter the WiFi password or network key.

Once you have done that tap 'join'.

Chapter 2: Setting up Your iPad

For your home WiFi, the network key or password, is usually printed on the back of your router.

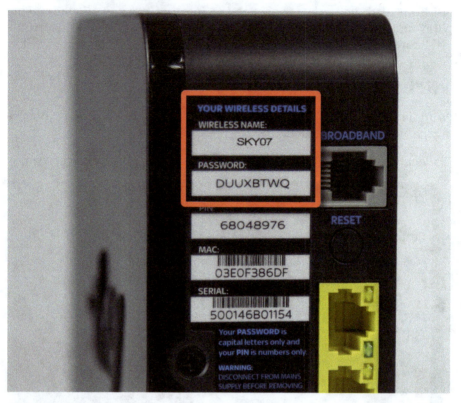

The network name is sometimes called an SSID.

Use the same procedure if you are on a public hotspot such as in a cafe, library, hotel, airport and so on. You'll need to find the network key if they have one. Some are open networks and you can just connect.

When using public hotspots, keep in mind that most of them don't encrypt the data you send over the internet and aren't secure. So don't start checking your online banking account or shop online while using an unsecured connection, as anyone who is on the public WiFi hotspot can potentially gain access to anything you do.

If you're really concerned about security or use your devices on public hotspots for work, then you should consider a VPN or Virtual Private Network. A VPN encrypts all the data you send and receive over a network. There are a few good ones to choose from, some have a free option with a limited amount of data and others you pay a subscription.

Take a look at www.tunnelbear.com, windscribe.com & speedify.com

Setting up Email Accounts

Tap the settings app icon on your home screen

Scroll down to 'accounts & passwords'.

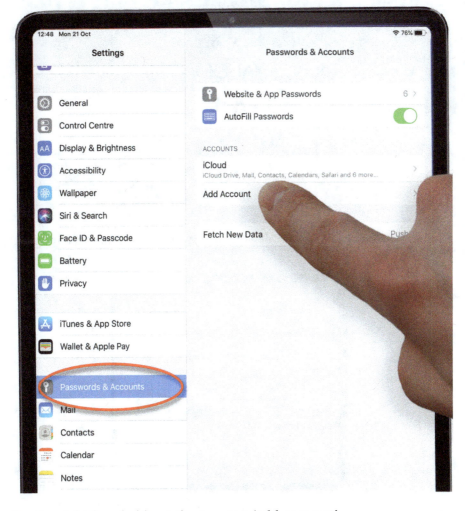

On the right hand side at the top, tap 'add account'.

Tap the type of account you want to add. If you have a Yahoo account, tap 'yahoo', if you have a Google/GMail account, tap 'google', or a Hotmail or Microsoft Account, tap 'outlook.com'.

In this example I am going to add a Microsoft Account. So I'd tap on 'outlook.com'.

In the box that appears, enter your account email address, tap 'next', then your password.

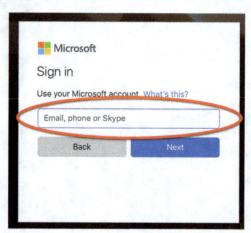

Tap 'next'.

Select 'yes' to the permission confirmation, to allow your iPad to access your email account.

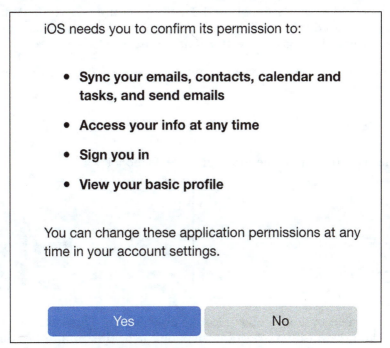

Select what you want your iPad to sync from the mail server. You can copy email, contacts, your calendar and any reminders onto your iPad by turning all the toggle switches to green, as shown below.

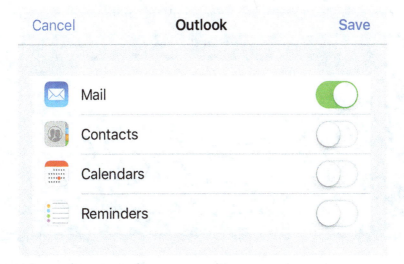

Tap 'Save'.

Add Social Media Accounts

You can add your Facebook and Twitter accounts to your iPad. The easiest way to do this is to go to the App Store and download the app for Facebook, Instagram, Twitter, and whatever else you use.

Tap on the 'app store' icon on your home screen. Tap 'search' on the bottom left.

In the search field on the top right type 'facebook'.

Tap 'get', next to the Facebook icon to download it. This icon might also look like a cloud if you have downloaded it before on another device, such as an iPod or iPhone.

Once the app has downloaded, hit your home button, then tap the Facebook icon on your home screen.

You can now sign in with your Facebook username and password.

You can use the same procedure to setup any other social media apps you want to use.

Change your Wallpaper

You can set a photograph as a background on your lock screen and home screen.

You can do this from inside the Photos App. Tap the photograph you want to set.

Tap the share icon on the top right of the screen. This will open up some sharing options along the bottom.

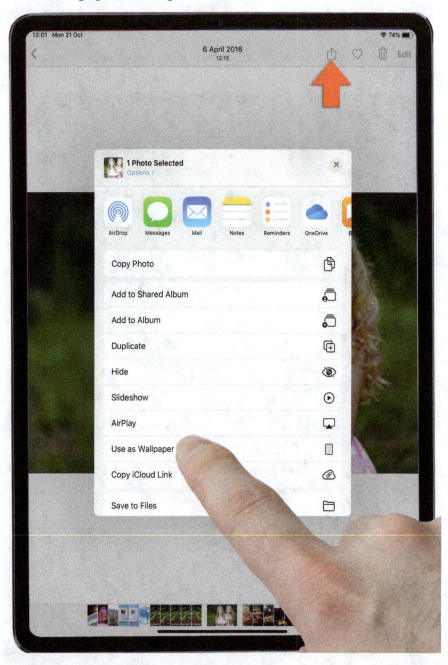

Scroll down, select 'use as wallpaper'.

Drag the photograph with your finger until it's in the desired position. You can also make the photograph smaller, by pinching the screen with your thumb and forefinger. Tap 'set' on the bottom right when you're done.

To set as both home and lock screen tap 'set both'. If you just want the photo on your home screen, tap 'set home screen'. Likewise for lock screen.

Dark & Light Mode

Introduced in iPadOS is a new dark mode. This reduces the amount of white on the screen and is perfect for low-light environments making it easier on your eyes.

To enable dark mode, open your settings app, and select 'display and brightness'.

On the right hand side, select 'dark' to switch to dark mode.

You can also set your iPad to switch to dark mode automatically. This means your iPad will switch to light mode during the day, and dark mode at night. To do this, tap the switch next to 'automatic'.

Tap 'options' to change when your iPad changes between dark and light mode. To set your own schedule tap 'custom schedule' and enter the times.

Touch ID

New iPad Pros no longer have a home button; they use face ID instead of Touch ID. Some of the older iPad Pro models have a home button, so we'll include this section for completeness. To set up Touch ID, open your settings app, tap Touch ID & Passcode. Enter your passcode when prompted.

Tap 'add fingerprint'.

Scan the finger you are most likely to use to press the home button with. In most cases this is your thumb, so it makes sense to scan this finger. Follow the instructions on the screen.

You'll need to scan your finger a few times, so the system can account for different variations, as you wont always put your thumb on the pad in exactly the same position every time. Do what it says on the screen. When you're done, tap 'next'.

Check out the Touch ID demo in the 'using iPad' section of the video resources on how to scan your fingerprint. Scan the code with your iPad or go to the following website

www.elluminetpress.com/using-iPad

Face ID

Face ID is used to unlock your iPad. To set up Face ID, open your settings app, tap 'Face ID & Passcode'. Enter your passcode when prompted.

Tap 'Set Up Face ID' or 'Enrol Face' if you're setting up another ID.

Look straight at your device then rotate your head around in a circular manner - looking left, looking up, looking right, looking down - almost like doing neck exercises, until the green marker makes it all the way around the circle. Tap 'done' to accept.

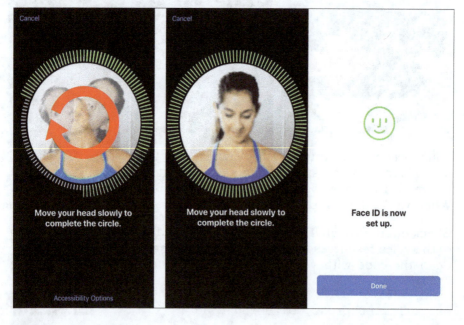

Sign in & Sign Out of iCloud

If you've set up your iPad from new and been through the initial setup, then your iPad will normally be signed in to your iCloud account. However if you need to sign into another iPad then you can do so from the settings app.

To **sign in**, open your settings app, tap on 'sign in to your iPad' then enter your Apple ID email address and password. Tap 'sign in'.

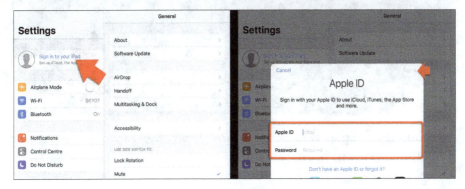

To **sign out**, open your settings app, tap on your Apple ID.

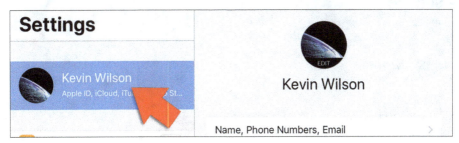

On the bottom right hand side, tap 'sign out'.

Pairing Bluetooth Devices

You can pair bluetooth keyboards, headphones, and bluetooth capable hardware in some cars.

To pair a device, first put the device into pairing mode. You'll need to refer to the device's instructions to find specific details on how to do this. On most devices, press and hold the pairing button until the status light starts flashing. This means the device is ready to be paired with your iPad.

On your iPad, open the settings app. From the settings app, select 'bluetooth'.

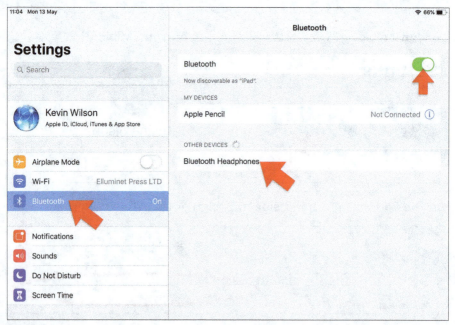

Turn it on, if it isn't already.

Your iPad will scan for devices nearby. You'll need to give it a few seconds to work. Any devices found will be listed. Tap on the device in the list to pair it.

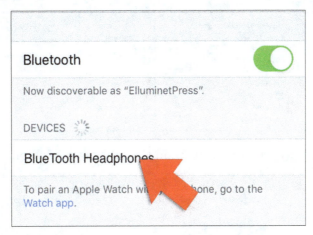

Some devices require a PIN code, enter it if prompted. Refer to the device's instructions to find out what the PIN code is. On most devices the default PIN is 0000, 1111 or 1234, but not always.

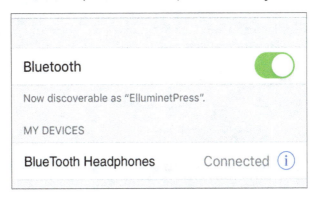

To remove a device, tap the 'i' info icon, then tap 'forget this device'.

Find My

This feature is quite useful if you have misplaced your iPad or had it stolen. You can also share your location with friends and family - a useful feature to keep track of where your kids are or family members.

Setup

First you need to activate it on your iPad. Tap the settings app, select your account, then tap 'find my'. Switch the 'find my ipad' slider to 'on'.

Tap on 'find my ipad', then turn on the other three switches.

Also make sure location services is turned on. To do this go back to the settings home page and select 'privacy'.

Tap 'location services', and turn the slider to 'on'.

Locating & Taking Action

On any device - iPad, Mac or PC, open your web browser and navigate to:

`www.icloud.com`

Sign in with your Apple ID. Select 'find iPhone' from the iCloud control panel.

You can locate your iPad. Select the name of your device from the drop down menu in the top middle of the screen.

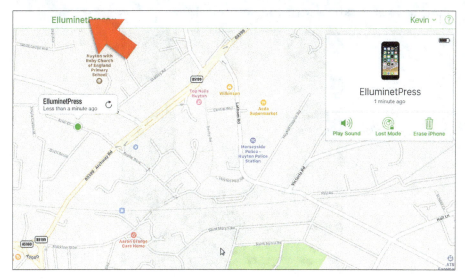

You'll see a green dot appear on the map. This is the current location of your device.

On the right hand side of the screen, you can take action. Here you can tap 'play sound' to play an annoying sound on your iPad wherever it might be. This helps you to locate it, if you've lost it in your house somewhere, or annoy a thief if they have possession of it.

You can also put the iPad into 'lost mode'. Lost mode allows you to remotely lock your device. You can also enter a message to display on the lock screen of the device.

Finally you can erase your iPad completely. To remove any personal data that is stored on your iPad.

Sharing Locations

You can share your location with friends and family. To share your location, open the 'find my' app then select 'people tab'.

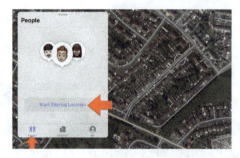

Select 'start sharing location' (or 'share my location' if you are already sharing your location with someone else).

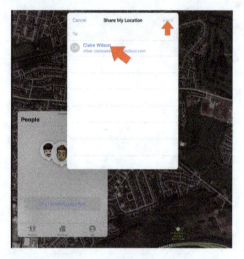

Enter the Apple ID or phone number of the person you want to share your location with. Tap 'send'.

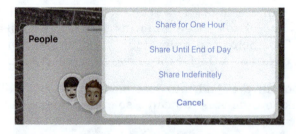

Choose to share your location for One Hour, Until End of Day, or Share Indefinitely. Tap OK.

The other person will get a prompt on their device. This will allow them to share their location with you.

Tap on the person's name on the people tab

You should see the person's location appear on the map on your device.

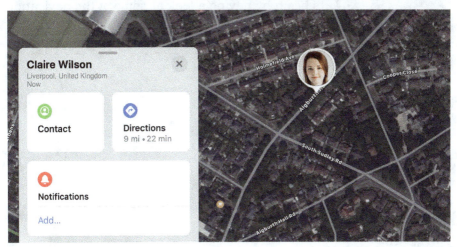

Tap 'contact' to send the person a message, tap 'directions' to see directions to the person's current location, tap notifications to add a notification when the person arrives at your location, leaves their location or any other location.

Chapter
3

Getting Around Your iPad

The iPad runs an operating system called iPadOS.

iPads have a touch screen user interface allowing you to interact with the apps on the screen using touch gestures.

We'll take a look at the different parts of the user interface, such as the control center, notifications and lock screen.

Lets begin by having a look at some of the navigation features of iPad. Take a look at the video resources

www.elluminetpress.com/ipad-pro-navigation

Home Screen

The home screen is a launch pad where you'll find icons for all your apps. With iPadOS, the home screen has a few improvements over previous versions. The app icons are now smaller giving more space for apps.

In horizontal mode, you now have the ability to pin widgets to the left hand side of your screen. This panel is called 'today view'.

Widgets

Widgets give you quick access to actions in your favourite apps, as well as information from other apps such as the weather, maps & traffic, calendar appointments and so on. Hold your iPad in horizontal mode, you'll see the 'today' view on the left hand side of the screen. If you don't see it, swipe right until the panel shows up.

To edit and add widgets, scroll down the 'today view' list, tap the edit button at the bottom.

Tap the red minus icon next to a widget you want to remove.

Tap the green plus icon next to the widgets you want to add.

Tap 'done' when you're finished.

Shortcuts

A shortcut is a quick way to execute tasks with your apps using one or more actions. An action is a single function within an app you can use in your shortcut such as send email to a group or open a web page. Each shortcut is made up of a series of actions. These shortcuts can either be triggered manually or you can be triggered by an event or at a particular time. This is called automation.

You will find the shortcuts icon on your home screen or on your 'today view'. This allows you to quickly access your shortcuts.

To create a shortcut, go to 'my shortcuts' then tap 'create shortcut'.

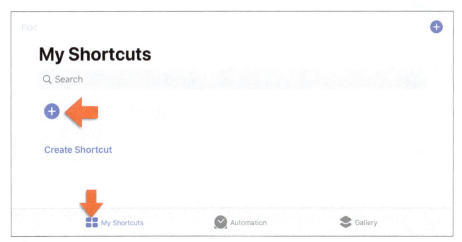

Chapter 3: Getting around Your iPad

From the left hand panel select the category of action you want to add.

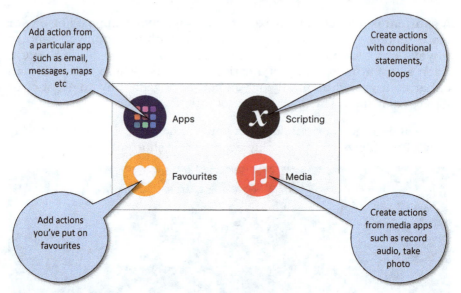

For this example, I'm going to use an app, so select 'apps'. Select the app you want to create a shortcut for. Eg 'mail'.

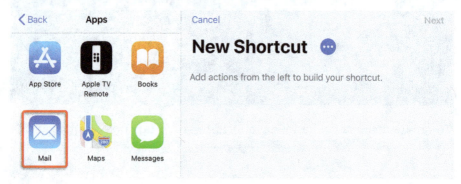

Say you wanted to be able to quickly send an email to a group of people - friends, colleagues, work groups etc. Tap 'send email'.

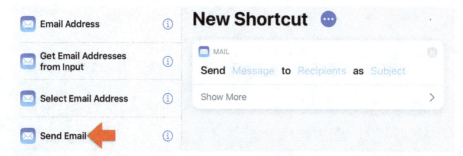

Now configure the shortcut. For this shortcut, I want a feature that will allow me to send an email to a specific group of people. Tap 'recipients'. Add the email addresses.

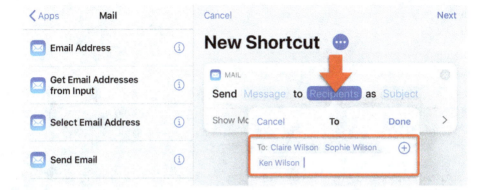

Tap 'next' on the top right. Give the shortcut a name. I'm calling this one 'production team'. Tap 'done'.

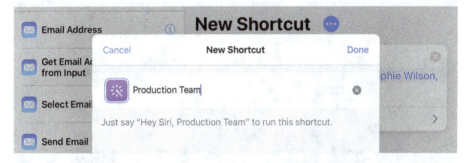

You'll find your new shortcut on your 'today view' panel on your home screen, or in the 'my shortcuts' view on the shortcut app.

Now, whenever I need to send an email to my production team, I just tap on this shortcut.

If you need to delete a shortcut, go to the shortcuts app, open 'my shortcuts', tap and hold your finger on the shortcut then tap 'delete'.

The Dock

The dock runs along the bottom of your screen, and is a place where you can access your most used apps.

You can also add your favourite apps to the dock at the bottom of the screen.

To do this, tap, and drag the icon to the dock.

Status Bar

The status bar runs along the very top of the screen. On the left hand side you'll see your clock and date.

On the right hand side you'll see your system icons for wifi, cellular, and remaining battery capacity.

Control Centre

The control centre is your control hub where you can adjust screen brightness, volume, access WiFi/bluetooth controls, access your camera, and other controls.

To open control centre, swipe downwards from the top right edge of your screen.

Here you can control the volume of playing music, turn on and off WiFi, blue-tooth, access your camera, set the orientation lock to stop the screen shifting - this can be useful if you are reading a book etc.

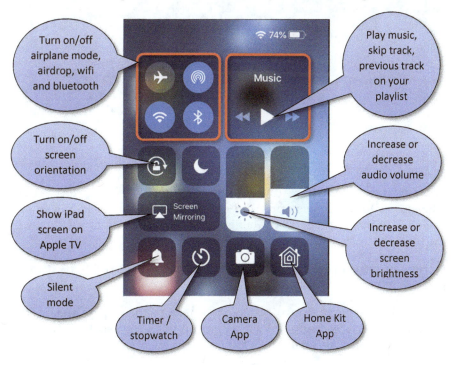

Customising Control Centre

To customise the controls, first open your settings app. Tap 'Control Centre' then tap 'Customise Controls'.

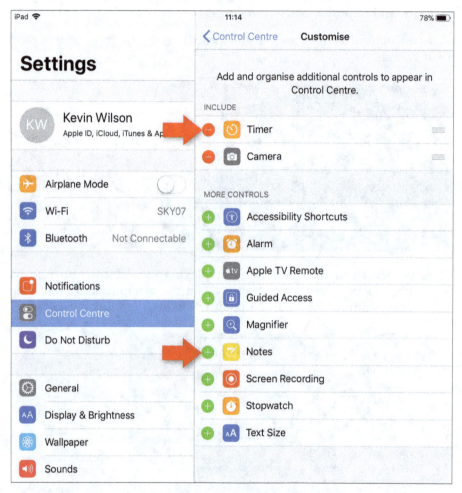

The settings for this are divided into two sections. The top section labelled 'include', shows apps and icons that will appear in the control centre. The bottom section labelled 'more controls', shows apps and features that are available but are not enabled.

To remove apps or icons from control centre, tap the red '-' next to the app name in the top section.

To add apps or icons, tap the green '+'next to the app in the bottom section. The enabled app or icon will jump to the top section, meaning it is now enabled and will show up on the control centre.

Notifications & Lock Screen

These two have now been merged. Swipe your finger downwards from the top centre edge of the screen, to invoke the lock screen & notifications.

Notifications such as email, sms/text messages or reminders can also appear on the lock screen.

Tap on one of the notifications to see more information.

Chapter 3: Getting around Your iPad

Tap 'view' to view the notification in full, tap 'clear' to remove the notification from your lock screen.

'Manage' allows you to change the notification settings for the app - eg you can turn off the notification for that particular app.

Tap settings and you can specify whether you want the notification to appear on lock screen & notification center, as well as what sound the notification makes when it pops up

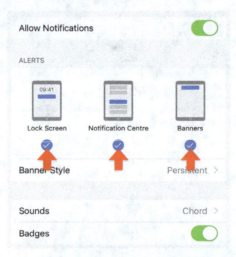

If you want the notifications to stay on your lock screen all the time, change 'banner style' to persistent. If you want the notification to popup, alert you, then disappear, change 'banner style' to temporary.

Touch Gestures

Gestures, sometimes called multi-touch gestures, are what you'll use to interact with the touch screen on iPad.

While you work through this part, take a look at the 'navigation' section of the accompanying video resources. Scan the code or go to the following website.

www.elluminetpress.com/ipad-pro-navigation

Tap

Tap your index finger on an icon or to select something on the screen. For example, you can tap on an app icon, a link in safari, or even a song you want to download.

You can also tap and hold your finger on the screen to access other options that might be available (this is like right-clicking the mouse on your computer).

Drag

Tap on the screen and without lifting your finger off the glass, slide your finger around the screen to drag up and down, left or right, and any other direction on the screen.

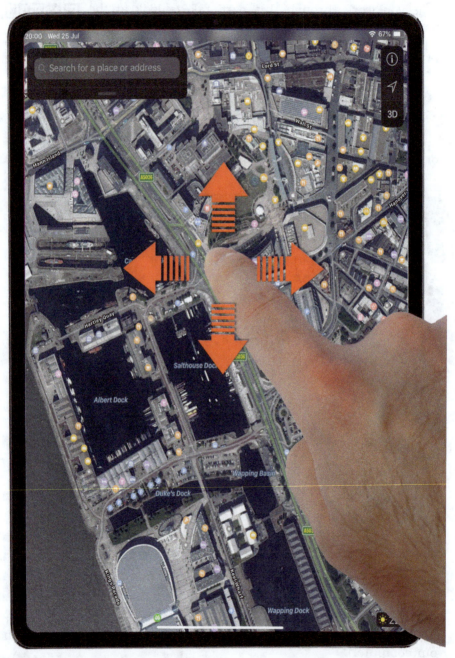

Pinch & Spread

Hold your index finger and thumb on the area you want to zoom in or out of, then pinch the screen to zoom out and spread to zoom in.

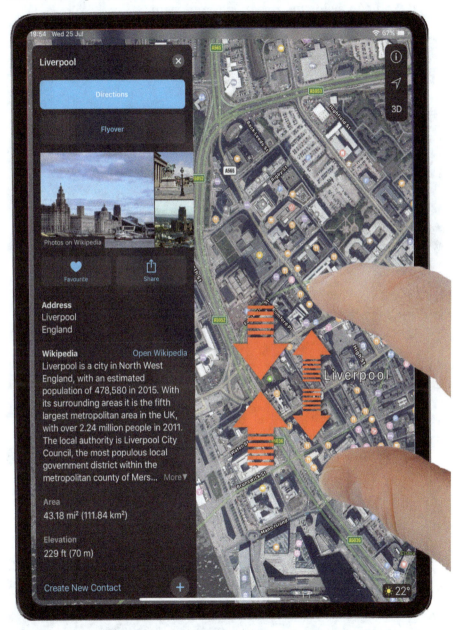

Pinch is shown in the illustration above, with the large red arrow, spread is shown with the small red arrow.

Swipe

This allows you to flip through photos, pages in an e-book, pages on the home screen. You swipe across the screen almost like striking a match. You can swipe up, down, left, and right.

Four Finger Swipe

Hold your four fingers (not your thumb) on the screen and swipe across to switch between open apps. You can swipe left and right.

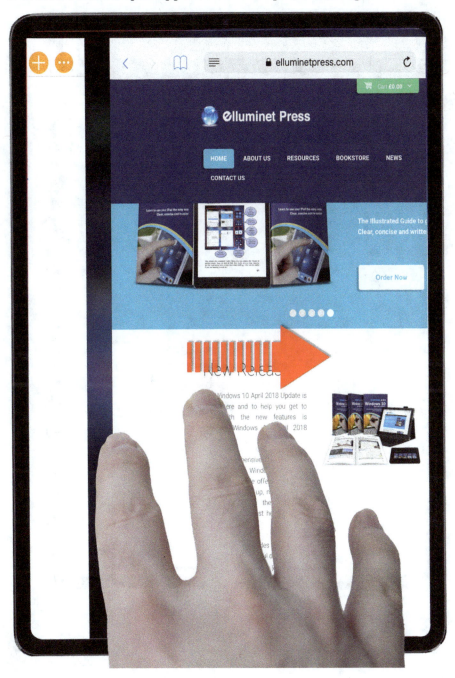

Reveal Home Screen

To reveal the home screen, swipe upwards on the home indicator bar on the bottom of the screen.

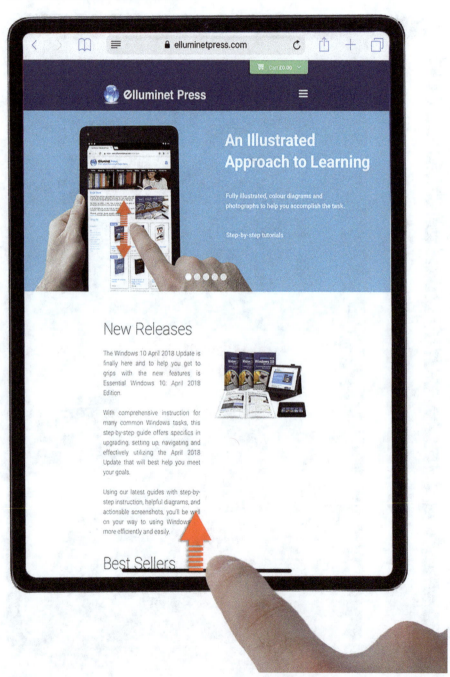

Reveal App Switcher

To reveal the task switcher, so you can see all your running apps, drag the indicator bar at the bottom of the screen upwards to the center of the screen, until the app thumbnails appear.

New Touch Gestures

Introduced in iPadOS are some new gestures. You can use these to copy and paste, as well as selecting text.

Cut, Copy & Paste

Select the text you want to copy or cut. To cut text, pinch with three fingers twice in a row. To copy text, pinch with three fingers once.

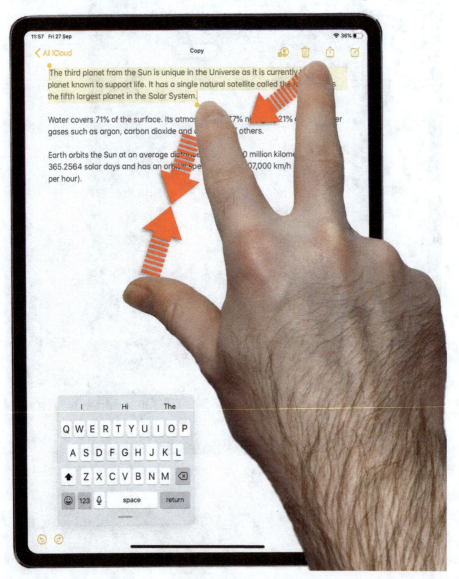

Pick up the cursor and drag it to where you want to paste the text.

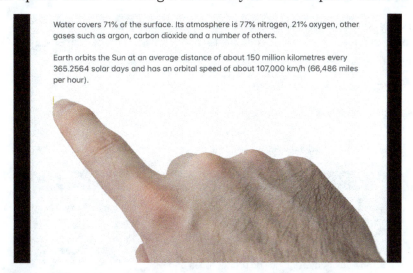

To paste text, spread with three fingers to paste.

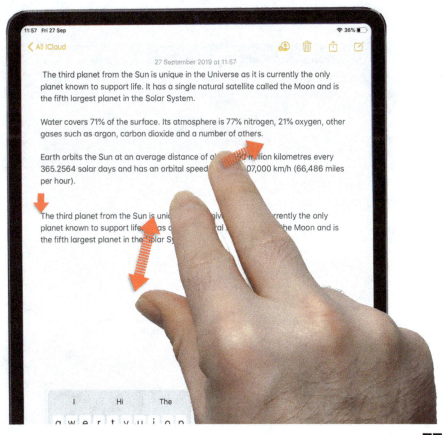

Text Selection

Quickly select a block of text by dragging your finger over it. You can also select a word with a double tap. A sentence with three taps. Or a whole paragraph with four taps.

To select a word, double-tap on it.

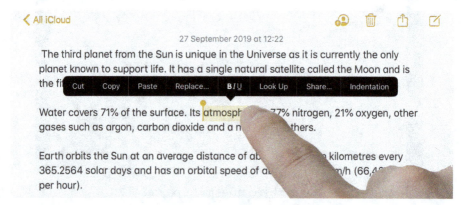

To select a sentence, tap on the text three times.

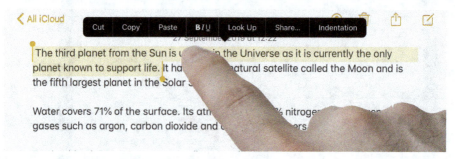

To select a paragraph, tap on the text four times.

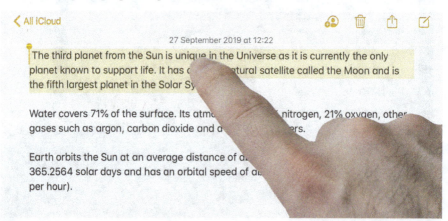

Multitasking

iPads run an operating system called iPadOS. iPadOS is a multitasking operating system. This means that you can run more than one app at the same time. Open apps that are not currently on your screen will be running in the background. To quickly see what apps are running, drag your finger upwards from the bottom edge to the center of the screen, until the app thumbnail icons appear.

Chapter 3: Getting around Your iPad

After using your iPad, you will find that there are a lot of apps running, this can severely affect the performance of your iPad and drain your battery more quickly.

To close apps, swipe your finger upwards on the app you want to close, as illustrated below.

This will close the app. Do this on all the apps you want to close.

You can also use this technique to switch between apps. Swipe your finger left and right to browse through the apps, then tap on the app you want to switch to.

Take a look at the multitasking demos in the 'using ipad' section of the accompanying video resources. Scan the code or go to the following website.

www.elluminetpress.com/using-iPad-pro

Open Multiple Apps at a Time

You can open multiple apps using two new methods. You can use slide over, where your app floats on top of the other and split view, where your apps run side by side.

Take a look at 'slideover feature' and 'splitscreen feature' demo of the accompanying video resources. Scan the code or go to the following website.

www.elluminetpress.com/using-ipad-pro

Using Slide Over

While running an app, swipe upwards from the bottom edge of the screen without lifting your finger off the glass to reveal the dock, then drag an app icon off the dock onto your screen.

Your app will open up and float on top of your screen.

You can interact with your app in the normal way and you can drag the app to either side of the screen. Use the small tab on top of the window to drag.

Multiple Apps in Slide Over

You can add more than one app to your slide over panel. Swipe up to reveal your dock, then drag the apps over to left.

Drag a second app and drop it on top of the previous app

Swipe Between Slide Over Apps

To reveal the apps you have open in the slide over panel, swipe upwards on the small tab at the bottom of the window.

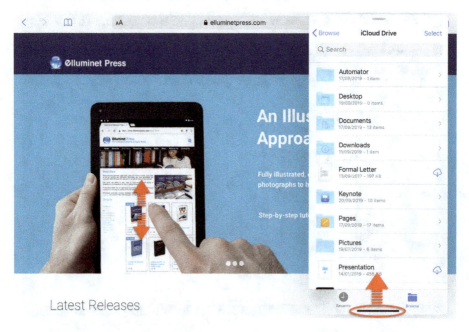

You'll see all the apps you have open in the slide over panel.

Tap on one of the apps to switch to it.

Using Split View

While running an app, swipe upwards from the bottom edge of the screen without lifting your finger off the glass to reveal the dock, then drag an app icon off the dock to the edge of the screen.

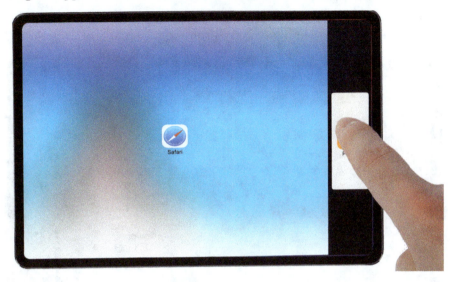

Your screen will split and you'll see one app on the left hand side and the app you just opened on the right.

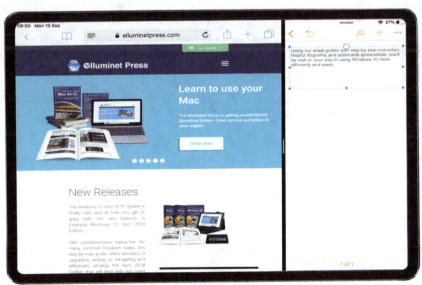

You can drag and drop information between the apps, as well as copy and paste information.

Drag & Drop

The Drag and Drop feature allows you to drag text, photos or documents from one app to another. You can drag items within the same apps or across different apps

In the demo below, the email app is running with files app running as a slide over app, as demonstrated in the previous section.

Tap and hold your finger on an item - photo or file, then drag your finger across the screen and drop the item where you want.

You can also drag and drop using the split view. Open the two apps in split view as demonstrated in the previous section.

In the demonstration above, I have the email app running in split view with the files app.

To attach the document to the email, tap and hold your finger on the document in the files app, then drag it across to the email app.

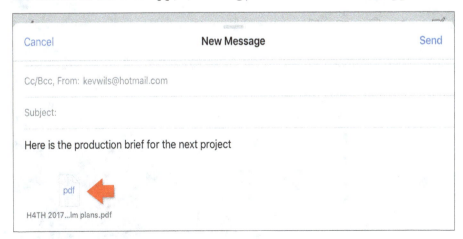

To close the slideover app, swipe the app off the edge of the screen.

To close your splitscreen, swipe the handle on the divider off the screen.

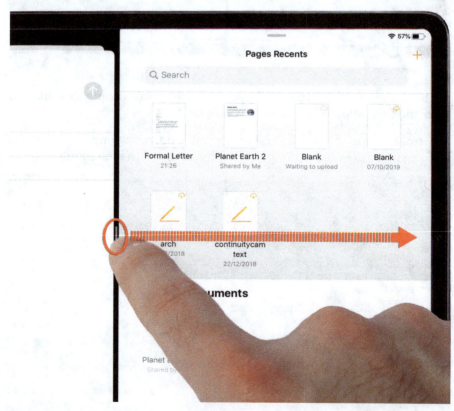

Picture in Picture

Picture in Picture is for video. This can be FaceTime video or a film from your video library. The video shows up as a small thumbnail that can sit over the other apps you're using.

Tap the little icon on the top left of the video window while watching a video on your video player, the video will turn into a thumbnail.

You can also drag the thumbnail into position. You can now go back to the home screen, open another app and the video will remain on top so you can see it while working on something else.

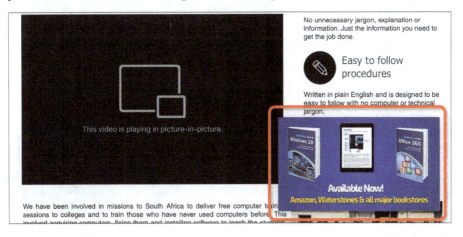

If you now go back to your home screen, the video stays in the corner

You can open any app and continue working. In this example, I am going to open the email app.

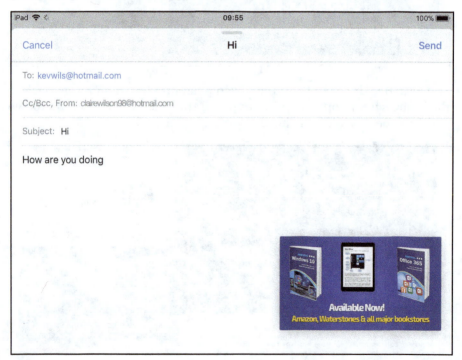

Handoff

Handoff allows users to share documents, e-mails, and websites over WiFi to your other devices.

For example, if you're typing an email on your Mac, you'll see an icon appear on the right hand side of the dock on your iPad.

Your iPad will allow you to pick up where you left off from the app you were using on your Mac. On your iPad, tap the icon on the right hand side of the dock to open the app.

You'll notice a small computer on the top right of the icon - this indicates a handoff app from another device.

Chapter 3: Getting around Your iPad

Once you tap on the icon, the app will open on your iPad allowing you to carry on from where you left off.

Handoff will also work the other way. If you happened to be out and about, and you started browsing the web, when you bring your iPad near your Mac, you'll see an icon on the left hand side of the dock...

Click on the icon to open the app to carry on with what you were doing on your iPad.

Sidecar

Sidecar allows you to use your iPad as a second screen on a Mac running MacOS Catalina. For Sidecar to work, both your Mac and iPad must be signed in with the same iCloud account. Both devices must also be connected using a USB cable or Bluetooth. Sidecar works with the latest Apple hardware, so some older iPads and Macs wont work. You'll need a Mac that is 'Late 2015 or newer'.

First, set up Sidecar on your Mac. To do this, click the system preferences icon on the dock, then select 'Sidecar'.

Click the 'connect to' drop down menu.

Select your iPad from the dropdown menu.

Chapter 3: Getting around Your iPad

Once your iPad connects to your Mac, you'll see an extended desktop on your iPad.

Let's take a look at Sidecar's interface on the iPad... Along the left hand side of the screen you'll see a toolbar.

You can quickly send apps to your iPad screen. To do this, click and hold your mouse pointer on the green expansion button on the left top of an app. From the drop down menu select 'move to iPad'.

If you use any graphic apps such as illustrator or photoshop, Sidecar allows you to use your iPad as a graphics tablet.

Load up your graphics program on your Mac, then send it over to your iPad using the feature above.

Now, with your pencil, you can draw directly onto the screen.

Chapter 3: Getting around Your iPad

You can arrange your displays. On your Mac, open the settings app, select display, then select the 'arrangement' tab.

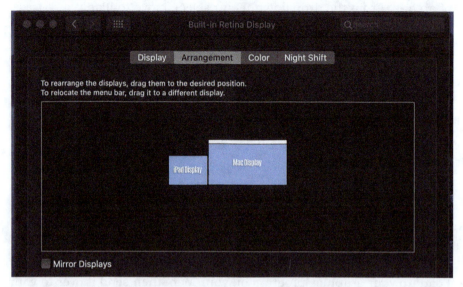

Your main laptop or mac display is represented by the large blue rectangle. Your iPad display is represented by the small blue rectangle.

If you use your iPad on the left hand side of your mac, move the small blue rectangle to the left of the large blue rectangle. If you use your iPad on the right hand side, move the small blue rectangle to the right. This makes it easier when dragging windows from your Mac to your iPad, so you drag them to the side of the Mac's screen on the same side as where your iPad is.

In the illustration, my iPad is on the left hand side, so I'd move the small blue rectangle to the left of the large blue rectangle. So now whenever I drag an app to my iPad, I drag it to the left where my iPad is physically.

The On-screen Keyboard

Typing on an iPad is easy, using the on-screen Multi-Touch keyboard. Tap in any text field, email, document or message, and the on screen keyboard will pop up on the bottom of the screen.

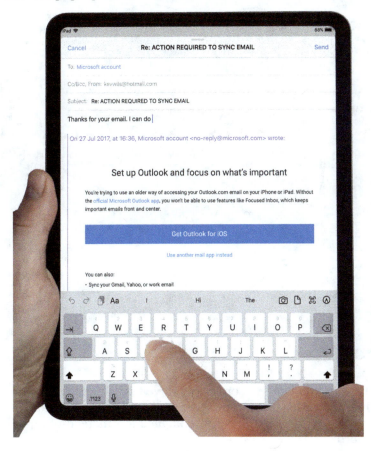

You can tap on the keys to type. To access the numbers and symbols on the top half of the key, tap and slide your finger down on the key. This is like holding down the shift key on a computer. For example, to type 4, tap and slide your finger down on the letter R.

Chapter 3: Getting around Your iPad

Lets take a closer look at the keyboard. You'll notice some icons and information along the top of the keyboard. Some of these will depend on which app you are typing in but most have a similar function.

Here is an example from the email app.

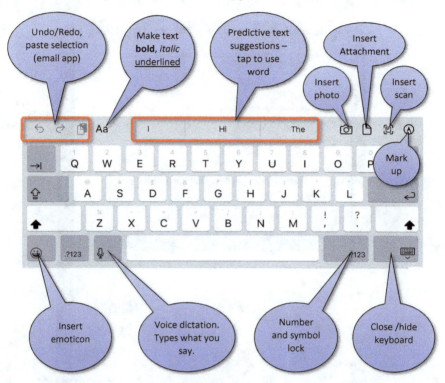

Along the top you will see some predictive text suggestions that appear according to what you're typing in. If the correct word appears, you can quickly tap on the appropriate suggestion instead of typing in the whole word.

On either side of the predictive text section, you'll see some app specific icons. These are usually shortcuts to common tools used in these apps. For example inserting photos or attachments in our email example or changing text to bold or italic.

Some icons along the bottom worth noting are: the '123' key, this locks in numbers and symbols so you can quickly enter a series of numbers just by tapping the keys. The 'smiley face' icon, these are emojis or emoticons - small smiley faces, thumbs up, expressions, and small images that are intended to show how you're feeling in your messages; happy, angry, amused and so on. Finally the 'microphone icon', this is a dictation tool that transcribes or types out voice dictations.

Apple Smart Keyboard

The smart keyboard is a keyboard built inside a folio case that your iPad slots into. You need to get the right size for your iPad and is either 11 inch & 12.9-inch iPad Pro.

The iPad slots onto the keyboard. Align the magnetic connector on the edge of the iPad to the dock connector on the keyboard. The cover attaches magnetically to the back of the iPad

Bluetooth Keyboards

You can also use any bluetooth keyboard. You can pick them up online or at any computer store.

To pair a bluetooth keyboard with your iPad, you'll need to put the keyboard into 'pairing mode' - see the instructions that came with your keyboard to find out how to do this.

Once your keyboard is in 'pairing mode', open the settings app on your iPad and tap 'bluetooth'. Turn bluetooth on if it isn't already.

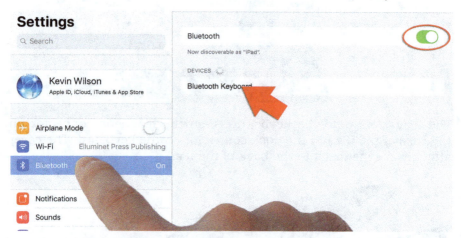

Tap the "Wireless Keyboard" device in the list of discovered bluetooth devices. You may need to wait a minute if it doesn't show right away.

On the keyboard, enter the 4-digit code that pops up on your iPad screen.

Once your keyboard has been connected or paired, you can type normally instead of using the on-screen keyboard.

This is useful if you are using Apple Pages to create a word processed document or typing an email, as the physical keyboard is much easier to use than the on-screen keyboard.

Mouse Support

You can use any bluetooth mouse. To enable mouse support, open your settings app, scroll down the left hand panel and select 'accessibility', then tap 'touch'.

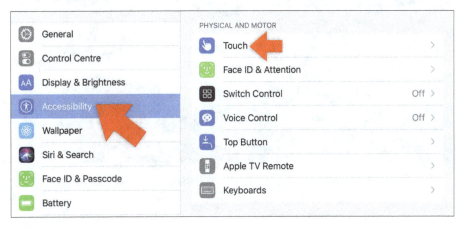

Turn on 'AssistiveTouch'.

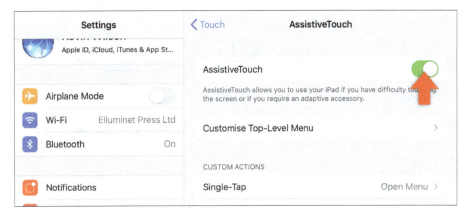

Scroll down and select 'pointer devices' then tap 'devices'.

Put your mouse into pairing mode.

Select 'bluetooth devices' to start the pairing process.

Your mouse will appear under the 'devices' section.

Tap on your mouse to pair it. You'll see a big black dot appear on your screen... this is your mouse pointer.

Tap 'AssistiveTouch' at the top of the screen to go back a page.

Under 'pointer devices', you can change the mouse pointer size.

Under tracking speed, you can change the speed of your mouse pointer.

Spotlight Search

Spotlight is integrated with a number of web services so that users can search using Wikipedia, Bing, or Google. Other services include: news, nearby places, suggested websites, movie show times, and content that is not already on the device from the iTunes Store

You can activate spotlight search by swiping your finger downwards from the centre of your home screen.

Once you have spotlight's search screen, you can type your search into the search field at the top of the screen.

Search also gives you some suggestions. These are listed below the search field and are the most commonly searched for entries for your search term. In the example below, I am searching for anything relating to 'computer'. Tap on the entry that best matches your search, or press enter on your on screen keyboard.

Scroll down the list to see files, apps, websites, news articles, and suggested websites according to your search terms.

Tap on one of the items to open it up.

You can track flights. This is a useful feature, especially if you have arranged to pick up a friend or collect a colleague from the airport.

If you have the flight number, enter it into spotlight search. There might be more than one flight, so make sure you confirm the correct departure and arrival times.

Tap on the flight to view tracking details. Here you'll see the current position of the aircraft on the map, which terminal the plane is arriving at and what time it is arriving - this plane is arriving at terminal 3 at 14:45.

Underneath you'll also see baggage claim timings and how long passengers are expected to get through. At the bottom you can find driving directions to the airport using the maps app.

Arranging Icons

To move an icon, tap and hold your finger on the icon, then drag your finger across the screen.

The other icons on the screen will automatically move and rearrange themselves around the icon you're moving.

To move the icon onto another page, drag the icon to the right or left edge of the screen. Once the icon page turns, release your finger.

You can get to the other pages by swiping your finger left and right to turn the page

The two little dots, circled in the illustration above, show you what page you are on and how many pages of icons you have. This will vary depending on what apps you have installed. In this example, there are two pages.

You can identify what page you are on by looking at this icon, the one in bold is the page you are on. In this example, page 1.

Take a look at the 'arranging icons' video demo of the accompanying video resources. Scan the code or go to the following website.

www.elluminetpress.com/ipad-pro-navigation

Removing Icons

This effectively deletes the app from your iPad. To do this, tap and hold your finger on the app's icon you want to delete, until you see a small x appear on the top left of the icons.

Tap on the x on the top left of the icon to delete it.

If you want to delete any other apps, tap the x on the icons. Press the home button when you're finished.

Siri

Siri is an extremely useful feature. She allows you to talk to your iPad, sometimes referred to as a virtual assistant; she can help you with all kinds of things. You can use Siri to send messages, schedule meetings, and search for nearby restaurants all without having to type a single letter.

Enable Siri

Check to see if Siri is enabled. To enable Siri, open your settings app

Select 'search & siri'.

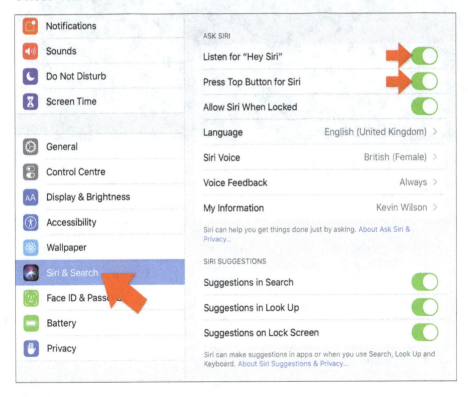

Turn on 'listen for hey siri', and follow the prompts to tune Siri to your voice.

Also, turn on 'press top button for siri'

Using Siri

To use Siri, press and hold power button on the top of your device until she appears. Then tell her what you need.

Try some of the following phrases...

"Hey Siri"

"Send email to..." (pick a name from your contacts list)"

"What is the weather like tomorrow"

"Find me a website on baking a cake"

"Remind me to pick up milk on the way home"

"Call..." (pick a name from your contacts list).

"How many kilograms are in a stone?"

"Make a note"

"What is ... address?" (add name of person or place)

"Launch maps"

Siri Translate

Here's a good one for those who love to travel but don't speak the local language. At the time of writing, Siri can only translate from US English to French, German, Italian, Mandarin and Spanish.

If you're using Siri with any language other than US English, you'll need to change this in the settings app. Tap 'Siri & Search', tap to change the language to 'English (United States)', circled below.

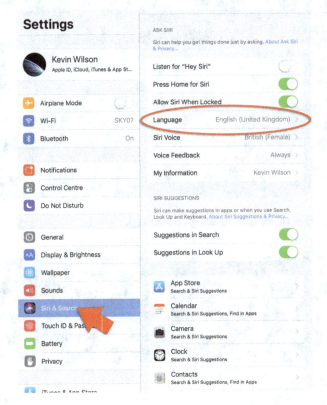

To use the translator, hold down the power button until Siri appears and speak the word **"Translate"**.

Siri will ask you which language you want to translate into. Say the language name or tap the option from the list. In this demonstration, I'm going to use Spanish.

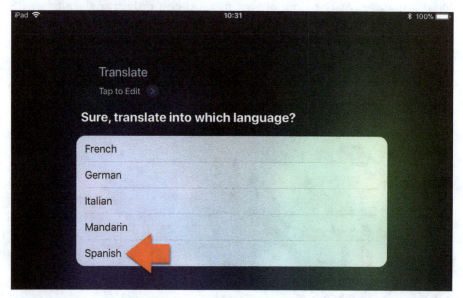

Now speak the phrase you want to translate into the language you just selected.

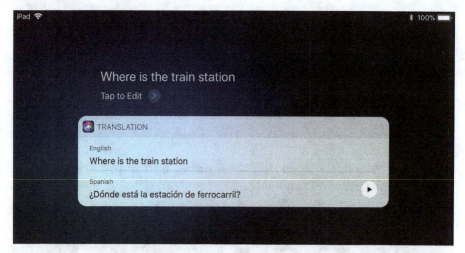

To play the translation again, tap the play button next to the translation.

You can also say "How do I say <u>where is the train station</u> in <u>spanish</u>?"

Just replace the underlined bits of the phrase for the phrase and language you want to translate into.

Voice Dictation

Another useful feature of Siri is voice dictation, which allows you to enter text without having to use the keyboard. You can search the web, take notes, post an update to Facebook, and more just by speaking.

To use voice dictation, tap the microphone icon on your on screen keyboard.

If the icon isn't there go to your settings app, tap 'general', then 'keyboard'. Go down to 'enable dictation' and switch the slider to on.

Then start dictating the text you want Siri to type. She listens to what you say, and types it. The more you use it, the better Siri gets at understanding you.

You can even add punctuation by saying words like "period" or 2 "question mark" when you reach the end of a sentence. Tap the keyboard icon on the bottom right to close dictation mode.

Voice Control

You can use voice commands to navigate around your device, launch apps and get things done without using your fingers.

To enable voice control, open your settings app then select 'accessibility'.

Select 'voice control', then tap 'set up voice control' at the top.

Tap 'continue'.

Have a look through all the voice commands you can give. Tap 'done' when you're finished.

Now, try a few voice commands. For example, say "open safari".

You can also customise commands. Open settings app, select 'accessibility', then select 'voice control'. Tap on 'customise commands'. To create a new command tap 'create new command'.

In the 'phrase' field, type in a phrase. This is the phrase you'll say to execute the command. Eg "Insert Claire's address". In the 'action' field, select the action this command is going to carry out. Tap 'insert text', then type in the text to be inserted. Eg an address. In the 'application' field, set this to any app, or tap and select the app you want the command to work in.

You can also record commands. Say "Start recording command". Perform the command on your iPad, then say "stop recording command", when you're done.

Settings Search

Tap on the settings app. On the main screen at the top left, swipe your finger down under the word 'settings'

This will reveal the settings search field.

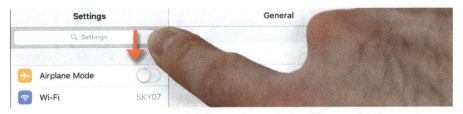

In the search field, type in the setting you want to change. I'm adding my email accounts so I'll type 'mail' in this example.

Tap on 'mail' to open mail app, or 'new mail' to open new mail message..

Family Sharing

You can now add six other users as family members. You can share iTunes and Apps, Apple Music, iCloud Storage, your location and authorize your kid's spending on the app store.

To set this up, go to settings and select your ID. Tap 'Set Up Family Sharing'. Then tap 'get started'.

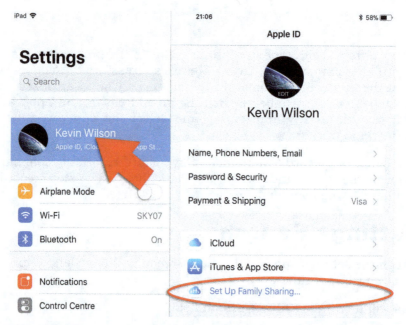

You'll see a screen with four options. You can share any of these options later on but this screen is asking which one you want to begin with. If you want to share books, apps, films and music; select the first option.

Tap 'continue' to confirm you want to use your Apple ID to share your purchases.

Confirm the payment details you want to share. Any member of your family that requests an app will be charged to this payment method on your approval. If you want to use another one tap 'use different payment method' and enter the card details.

Tap 'continue' if you want to use your default Apple ID payment method.

Tap 'invite family members'. Select 'invite in person' and enter their Apple ID email address. If they don't have an email address or too young, tap 'create a child account'.

Add a Family Member

Go to settings, select your ID. Tap 'family sharing then tap 'add family member'.

Now select how you want to invite them. You can invite then 'in person', ie enter their Apple ID email address, send an invitation via iMessage or 'create a new child account'.

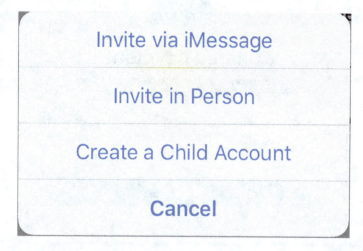

In this example I'm going to invite in person as this person is in the same house hold.

Invite in Person

Select 'invite in person' from the popup. Enter the person's Apple ID email address and password. If their details are in your address book, you'll see a suggestion underneath. Tap on the name if it's correct.

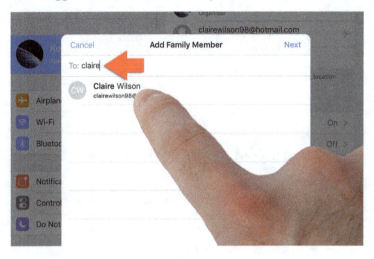

When the person signs into their iPad and checks their email, they'll see an invitation to join the family.

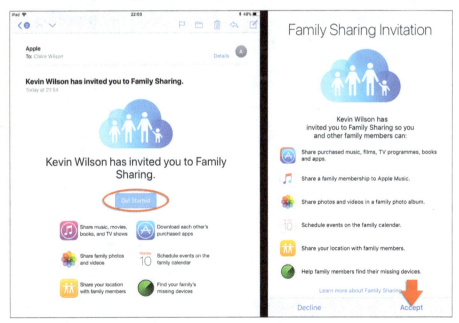

Click 'get started', then click 'accept' on the confirmation.

Child Accounts

If you have young children it makes sense to create separate accounts for them rather than allowing them to use yours. This helps to protect them and to help you monitor what your child is up to.

To create a child account, go to settings, select your ID. Tap 'family sharing' then tap 'add family member'. From the popup select 'create child account'.

Now follow the instructions on screen. Tap 'next' on the top right of the screen.

Enter your child's birthday using the rollers on the bottom of the screen, then tap next.

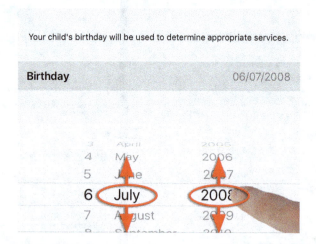

Agree to the disclosure, tap 'agree'.

Enter your CVV code from the credit card you have registered with your Apple ID. Tap 'next'.

Enter your child's first and last name using the on-screen keyboard, then tap 'next'.

Enter an Apple ID email them. Tap 'next'.

Enter a password for them and tap 'next'.

This will create a new account for your child to use.

Now, select some security questions that you will remember the answers to. This is a security step that will be used to identify you when you need to change a password or recover a forgotten password.

Select a question from the 'question' field and type in an answer in the 'answer' field. Tap 'agree' to accept the terms and conditions

Enable 'ask to buy'. This means that if your child tries to buy an app from the app store, a music track, tv show or film, you will receive an authorisation request where you can approve the purchase or deny it. Tap 'next'.

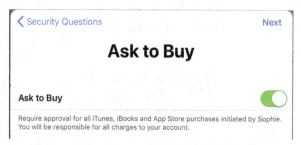

Now allow your child to sign into their iPad with the Apple ID email address and password you just created. In this example it would be sophie20077@icloud.com

Managing your Family

Family members can share purchased apps, music, and books using the same credit card. iPad can also automatically set up photo streams for all family members. Calendars may be synced between all members.

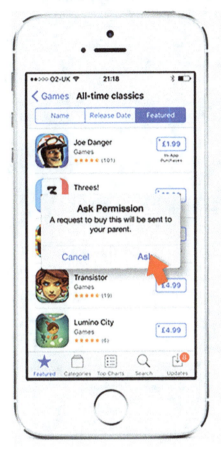 

Kids can also send iTunes and App Store download requests for apps, music, movies, and more to their parents provided this service is set up correctly.

On your device, tap 'review' from the prompt to see details of the request.

Screen Time

Screen Time collects usage statistics on the various apps you use on your iPad. It records how much time you've spent using a particular app, can generate activity reports, allows you to set app time limits, and can be useful for monitoring your kid's activity.

You can find screen time on your settings app. On the left hand side of the settings app, select 'screen time'.

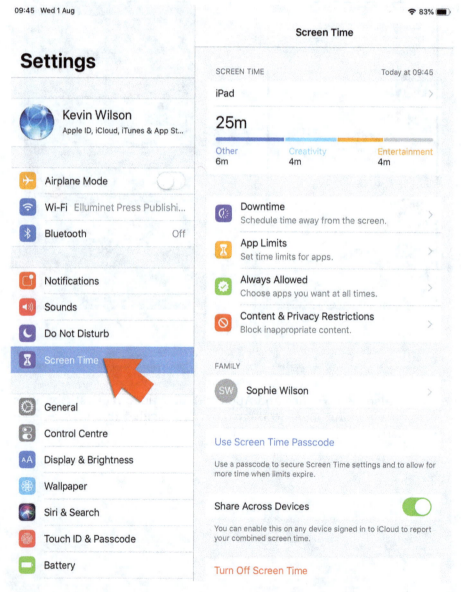

Lets take a look at the main screen.

Breakdown of usage stats of apps used on your iPad

Set a period of time when your apps will be unavailable

Add time limits to specific genres of apps. Eg 1 hour for games

Add apps that are allowed to run regardless of set limits

Allow or block certain content or apps. Eg age appropriate films

Set a passcode to prevent users from changing screen time restrictions

Starting from the top of the screen, you'll see a breakdown of the total time spend using your iPad

Below that, you'll be able to make some adjustments to the settings as shown in the image above.

From here, you can also block different apps and various web sites and content.

Downtime

With downtime, you can set a period of time, say a couple of hours, that your iPad apps are unavailable.

Select 'downtime' from the main screen, and turn it on using the switch at the top.

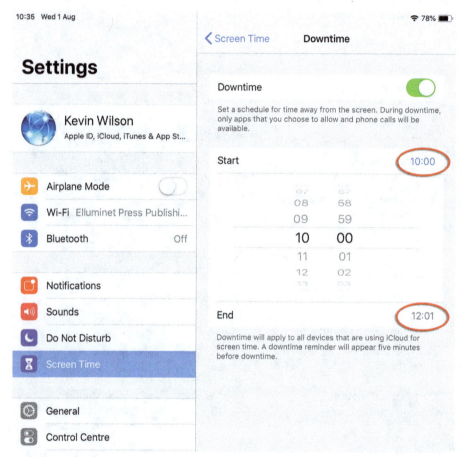

Below, you'll see two options appear. Use this to set the start and end times you want apps to be unavailable. Tap on the times to change them.

For example, you could set it from 9pm to 7am. This would mean, from 9pm, your iPad apps will turn off until 7am the next morning - preventing you from using your iPad late at night.

You could also set a limit so if your children use the iPad, they can't use it until a certain time - perhaps after they've done their homework.

App Limits

You can set the length of time you want a particular app to be available. To do this, select 'app limits' from the main screen, then tap 'add limit'.

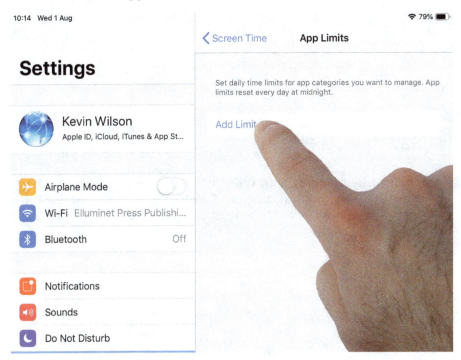

Choose the genre of apps you want to add the limit to. In this example I'm adding a limit to all social networking apps such as facebook, instagram and so on, then tap 'add'.

Set the length of time using the sliders indicated with the red arrow.

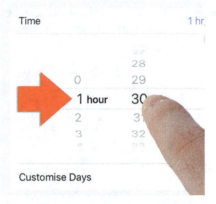

If you want different times on different days, select 'customise days'. This will allow you to input different time limits on different days. Eg, you might want to allow more time at the weekends. Tap on the time limits to change them.

< Back	**Customise Days**
Sunday	5 h
Monday	3 hr
Tuesday	3 hrs, 2
Wednesday	3 hrs, 2 min
Thursday	3 hrs, 2 min
Friday	3 hrs, 2 min
Saturday	5 hrs, 2 min

Tap 'back' to return to the previous screen.

< App Limits	**Social Networking**
Time	1 hr, 30 min

Tap the set time on the top right to confirm.

Always Allowed

This allows you to choose the apps you want to be available regardless of any content restrictions or time restrictions that are set. Tap the green + to add an app from the list, or tap the red - to remove an app.

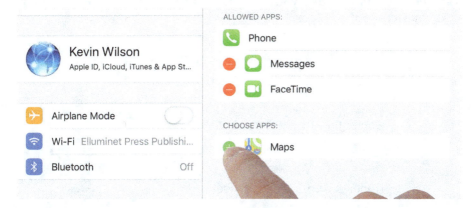

Content & Privacy Restrictions

Content & Privacy allows you to set restrictions on certain content such as age appropriate films and television programs, or songs, websites, and books with adult themes. This is useful if your kids are using the iPad.

To set content & privacy restrictions, from the settings app, on the screen time page, select 'content & privacy restrictions'.

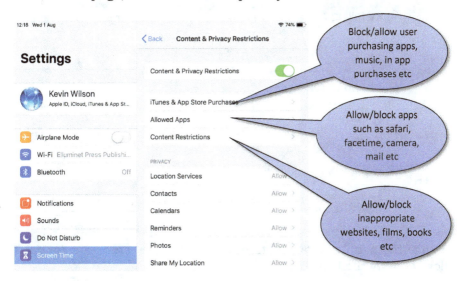

Allowing and Blocking Content

Go to the 'content & privacy restrictions' section of screen time. From here you can add restrictions on content, apps and websites.

Tap the options to make your selections about what content to allow and what content to block.

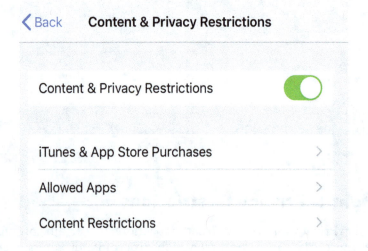

For example, to allow or block app store purchases, tap 'iTunes & App Store Purchases'

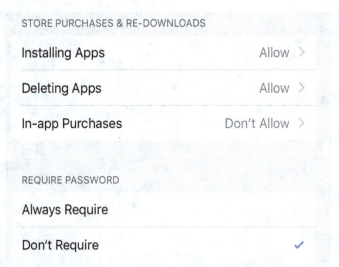

Change the setting to 'allow' to allow the feature, change it to 'don't allow' to deny the feature.

You can do the same for content restrictions such as age appropriate apps, films and websites.

To change these settings, tap 'content restrictions'

ALLOWED STORE CONTENT

Ratings For	United Kingdom >
Music, Podcasts & News	Clean >
Music Profiles & Posts	On >
Films	PG >
TV Programmes	Allow All TV Programmes >
Books	Clean >
Apps	12+ >

WEB CONTENT

Web Content	Limit Adult Websites >

SIRI

Web Search Content	Allow >
Explicit Language	Don't Allow >

Tap on and change the settings appropriately. For example, to only allow PG rated films, tap 'films' and select 'PG'

Do the same for websites, web search content and language. Tap and set these to the appropriate settings, as shown in the example above.

Internet, Email, Communication

Your iPad has a lot of features that allow you to connect to the internet, browse the web, send and receive emails, share pictures with friends, store addresses and contacts, have video chat conversations with friends and family.

To do this, Apple have provided some built in apps: Safari for web browsing, Mail for email and Face Time for video chat.

You also have apps for social media, and an address book to keep track of contacts addresses and details.

Lets start by taking a look at Safari web browser. Take a look at the video resources.

www.elluminetpress.com/ipad-pro-comms

Using Safari

To launch safari, tap on the safari icon located on your dock.

This will launch safari. Lets take a look at the main screen.

In safari's main screen, tap in the website address field, to enter the website's address, or Google search keyword.

Chapter 4: Internet, Email & Communication

Two menus to take note of. The first menu is on the left hand side of the screen and allows you to access favourite or bookmarked sites. You can tap on any of these in the list to return to the sites.

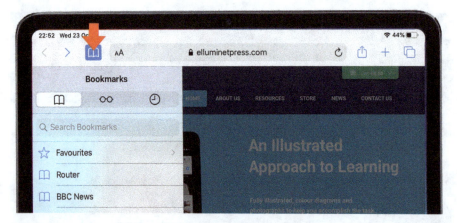

The second, is on the right hand side and allows you to share the current website link via text message, email or social media. Just tap on the icon to share the site on twitter or facebook, email the link or send it via text.

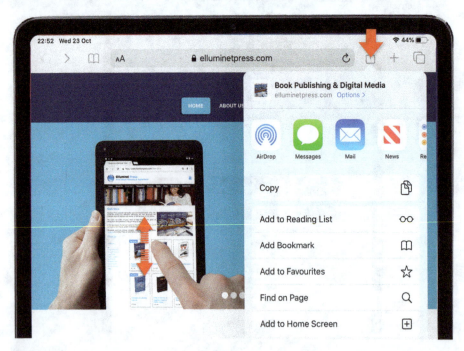

Along the bottom of that menu, you can add the current site to bookmarks/favourites. To do this tap bookmark.

Hit the + sign to add a new tab where you can open another website, Google search, favourite and so on.

The final icon on the right hand side, allows you to see all the tabs you currently have open

Safari will display your open tabs/websites as thumbnail previews, you can tap on to open up.

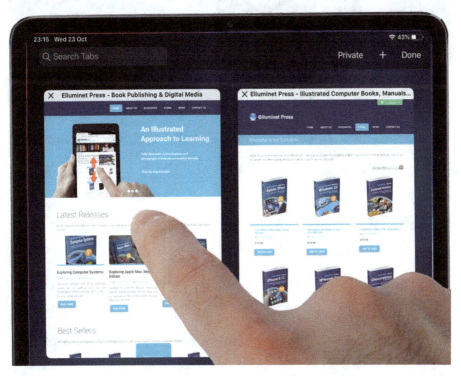

Bookmarking a Site

Bookmarking sites makes it easier to find websites that you visit most often, without having to search for them or remember the web address. To bookmark the site you're on, tap the sharing icon on the top left of the toolbar.

From the popup menu, tap 'add bookmark'.

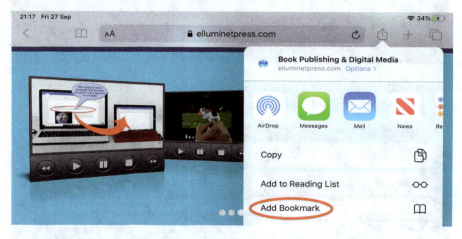

Enter a meaningful name if required as indicated below, then tap 'save'.

Tap 'favourites' under 'location' to select a folder to save your bookmark into. Select 'bookmarks'.

Revisiting a Bookmarked Site

You'll find all your bookmarked sites on the reading menu. To access this menu, tap the icon on the toolbar along the top left of the screen.

From the slideout panel, select the bookmarks icon.

You'll see a list of sites you have bookmarked. Tap bookmark to revisit site.

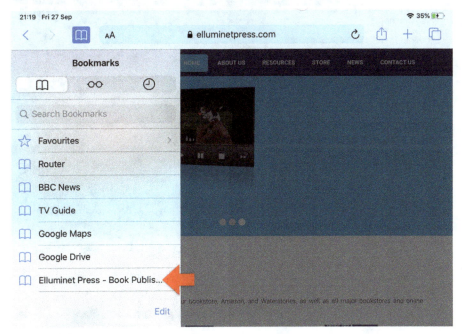

To Delete: Swipe right to left across the bookmark, and tap delete, to remove a bookmark.

To edit a bookmark, tap 'edit' on the bottom right corner, then tap on the bookmark in the list you want to edit. You can enter a new name, or change the web address.

137

Browsing History

Safari keeps a list of all the websites you have visited in the browser history. To view the history, tap the reading menu icon on the toolbar at the top left of the screen.

Tap the history icon from the icons at the top of the slidout panel.

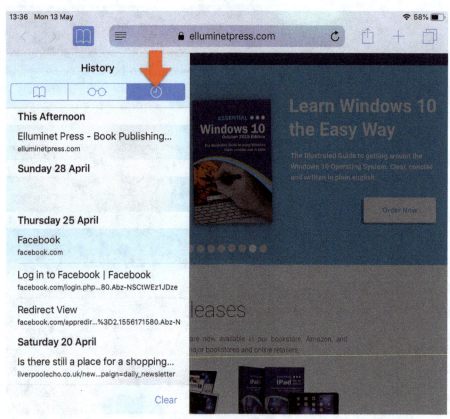

Scroll down the list, tap on a site to revisit.

Swipe right to left over the site in the list and tap delete, to remove the site from the history.

Tap 'clear all' on the bottom right to clear the entire history.

Reader View

Reader view makes it easier to read web pages without all the unnecessary background clutter that usually comes with a website.

Reader view is not available on all web pages but is on most. To enable reader view, tap the 'AA' icon on the left hand side of the web address search field. From the menu, select 'show reader view'.

Here below, you can see the normal view on the left and reader view on the right.

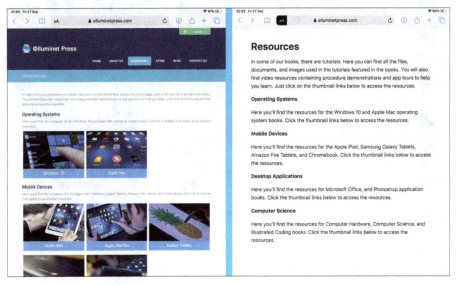

The reader view is designed to improve readability on screen and often removes a lot of graphics, photos and other media, so it's worth keeping this in mind if you are visiting media rich websites.

To go back to normal view, tap the 'AA' icon, then 'hide reader view'.

Check out the safari demos in the 'internet & email' section of the accompanying resources. Scan code or go to following website.

www.elluminetpress.com/ipad-pro-comms

Page Zoom

You can quickly zoom in and out on a website's text. To zoom in, spread your thumb and forefinger apart across the glass. To zoom out, pinch your thumb and forefinger together.

You can also control the text size and zoom using the 'AA' icon on the top left of the address field.

Tap the 'A' icons to decrease or increase the size.

Download Manager

When you download a file in Safari, a new icon will appear on the toolbar. Tap this icon to see your downloads.

You'll see the status of files you're downloading, as well as files you've downloaded. You can tap on the filename to open the file, or tap the magnifying glass icon to open your downloads folder

You'll also find your downloads folder in the files app. Here you'll find all the files you've downloaded.

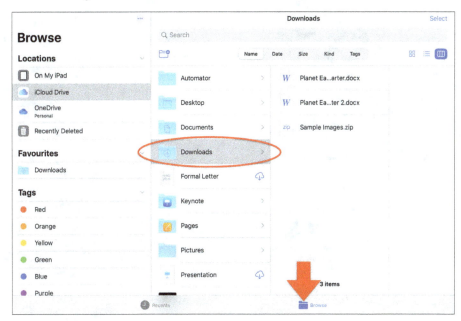

Generate Automatic Strong Passwords

Tap Safari and go to a website where you need to sign up for an account. In this example I'm creating a new Gmail email account.

Input a username or email address into the first field.

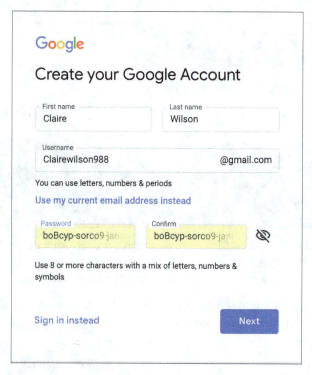

Tap on the password field. Safari will generate an automatic strong password for you.

Tap 'Use Strong Password' to store it in your keychain.

Autofill Passwords on Websites

Tap Safari and go to a site that you already have an account with. Eg the Gmail account we created earlier. Select the text input field for the username or email address associated with the account.

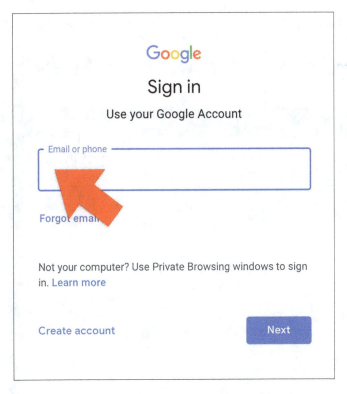

In the suggestions on the keyboard below, select "for this website". Authenticate the action with your Touch ID, Face ID, or passcode when prompted.

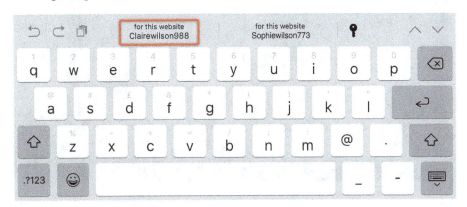

Automatically add Password to Keychain

When you sign into a website or for the first time, you will receive a prompt asking you whether you want to save your login details to keychain.

Tap Safari and navigate to the website you want to sign into. In this example, I'm signing into a facebook account.

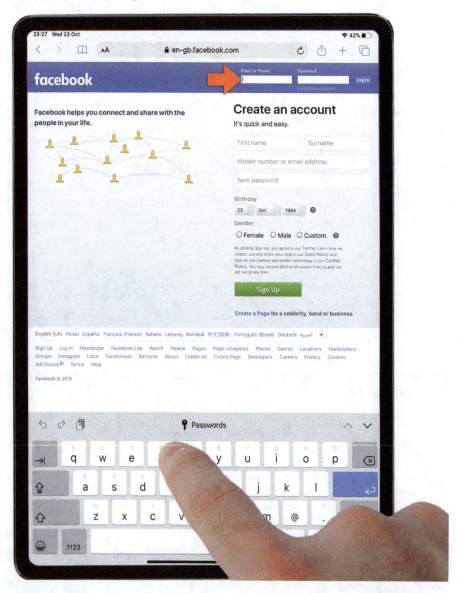

Sign in, in the normal way - enter your username and password.

Once you sign in successfully, Safari will prompt you to save the password to your keychain.

This will save your password so you don't have to type it in each time. To sign in the next time, just click in the username or password field.

Select the password from the suggestions along the top of your keyboard

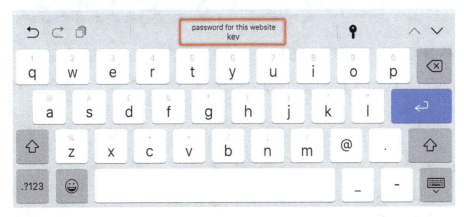

Tap the password suggestion from the options on the top of your keyboard. If your password isn't there, tap the key icon then select the password from the list.

145

Using Email

To start the mail app, tap Mail on the bottom of the screen.

Once your email is setup it will open on the main screen. The email app works best if you use your iPad in horizontal orientation. On the left hand side, is a list of all your emails. Just tap on one to view.

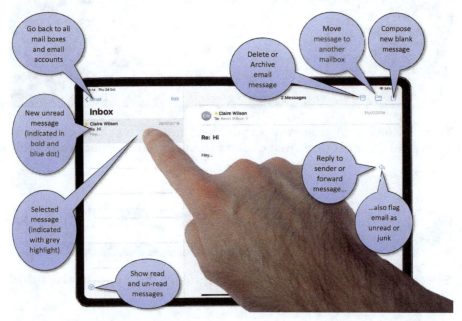

Reply to a Message

To reply to an email, select the email you want from your inbox, then tap the 'reply to sender' icon on the bottom right.

Tap 'reply' to reply to the sender, tap 'reply all' to reply to sender plus any other recipients who were copied in, tap 'forward' to send the message to someone else. Tap 'delete' to delete the email.

New Message

To send a new message, click the 'compose new email' icon on the top right. This will bring up a new email. Tap in the 'To:' field to enter an email address. If you are replying to a message, the email address of the person that sent you the message will appear here automatically.

Tap in the subject field and add some text.

Tap in the message body underneath and type your message using the pop up on screen keyboard.

If you look on the top of the on screen keyboard you'll see some icons.

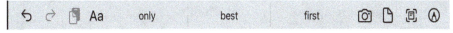

On the left, you can undo/redo text - undo is a good one if you make a mistake with your typing. You can also paste some text or an image you have copied from somewhere else. Next is the format icon, you can change your text to bold, italic or underlined. In the centre you have some text predictions - this shows up words you're most likely to type while writing your email - tap word to insert into message. You can insert a photo directly from your camera, and add an attachment, scan or markup.

Formatting Messages

A new menu adds comprehensive text formatting tools to help you compose better looking emails.

To use the formatting tools, tap the 'AA' icon on the top left of the on-screen keyboard to open the menu.

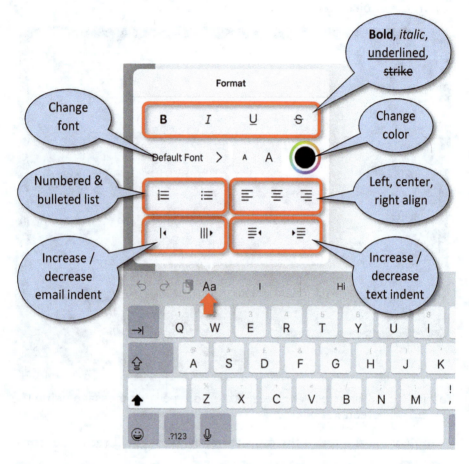

Select the formatting tool you want, then type your text.

Formatting includes new font style, size and colour selections, strikethrough, alignment, numbered and bulleted lists, and indenting options.

If you want to indent text use the 'increase/decrease text indent' icons. Increase/decrease email indent is for indenting parts of an email from someone you're replying to.

Attachments

To add an attachment such as a document, tap the document icon on the top right of the on-screen keyboard.

From the popup dialog box, select the document you want to attach to your email.

If you document isn't in the list, click 'see all' on the top right.

To add a photo, click the camera icon on the top right of the on-screen keyboard instead. Select 'photo library' to select a photo from your photos app, or tap 'take photo' to take a new one.

Check out the email demos in the 'internet & email' section of the accompanying resources. Scan code or go to following website.

www.elluminetpress.com/ipad-pro-comms

Flagging Messages

You can choose from a variety of colours when you flag an email message. Coloured flags are synced with iCloud to the Mail app on all your Apple devices.

To flag a message, open it up and tap the reply icon on the bottom right, then tap 'flag'. You'll see a small panel open up with different colours. Select one.

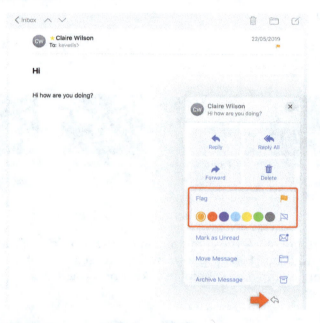

Block Sender

You can have email from a specified sender blocked and put directly to the trash. Blocking a sender works across all your Apple devices. First, open the message, tap the sender's email address at the top. Select 'Block This Contact' from the drop down.

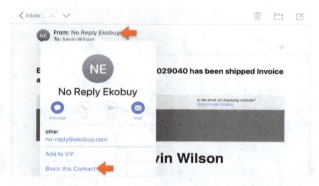

Contacts

The Contacts App is your address book. It contains all the names, email addresses, phone numbers and addresses of the people you correspond with.

To launch your contacts app, tap the icon on the home screen.

This is the main screen. You can browse contacts, or add new ones.

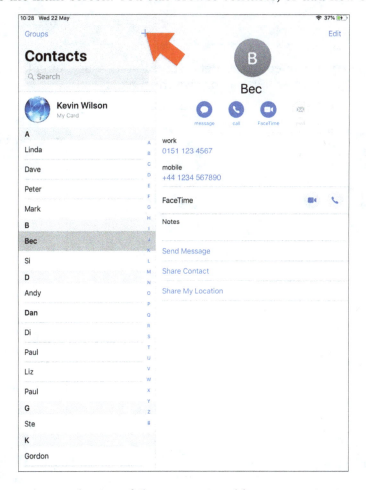

Tap the + sign at the top of the screen to add a new contact.

View Contact Details

To view a contact's details, tap on the name in the contacts list on the left hand side.

From here you can edit their details, send a message, email, FaceTime them if they have an iPhone, or give them a call.

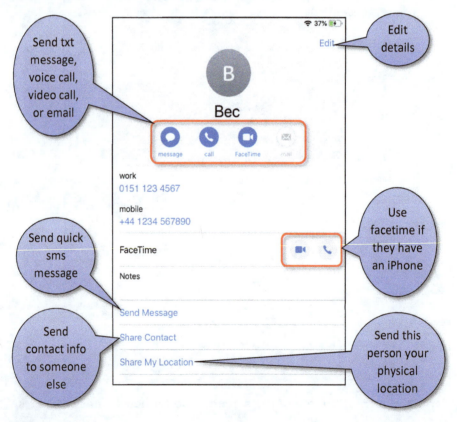

New Contact

Tap on the + sign on the top right of the main page to add a new contact.

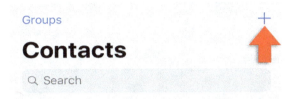

On the screen that appears, enter the person's name and contact details in the fields.

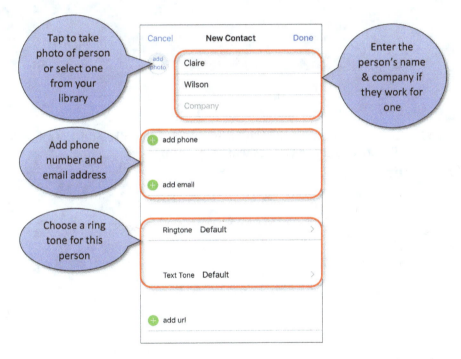

Add a profile photo. This photo appears on your phone screen when the person calls. To take a photo tap 'take photo', you can either take one with your camera or select one from your photo library.

Add their phone number, and email addresses in the relevant fields.

Choose a specific ring and text tone for this person. This is the sound you'll hear when this person sends you a message or calls you.

Tap 'done' on the top right when you're finished.

New Contact from a Message

You can also add a contact from an email message. Open the email message in the Mail App. Tap 'details'.

Tap on the person's name at the top of the email.

Tap 'create new contact'. Your iPad will automatically add the names and email address the message was sent from.

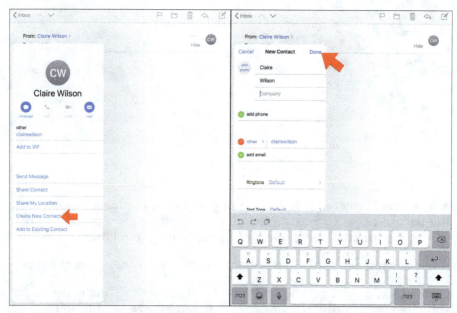

Add any other details if necessary. Tap 'done' when you're finished.

You can do the same with text messages in iMessage. Tap on the message, then tap 'details', tap the 'i' icon (top right), tap 'create new contact'. Enter their name and details in the screen that appears.

Delete a Contact

To delete a contact, open your contacts app and select the person's name in the list on the left hand side.

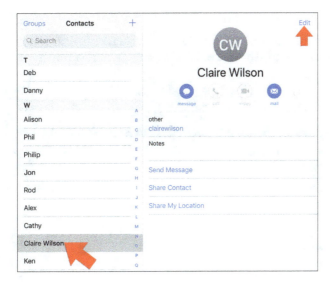

Scroll down the right hand side of the page, then click 'delete contact'

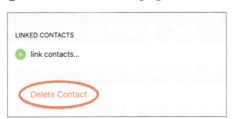

Check out 'adding contacts' and 'contacts from email message' demos in the 'internet & email' section of the video resources.

Scan the code with your iPad or go to the following website.

www.elluminetpress.com/ipad-pro-comms

Calendar (iCal)

To start calendar app, tap the icon on the home screen

This will bring up the calendar main screen. I found it easiest to view the calendar in month or week view. Below is in month view.

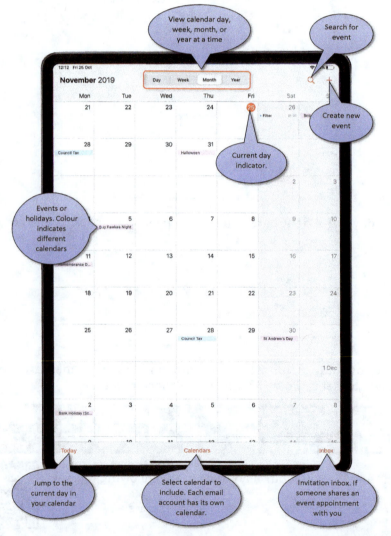

Adding an Appointment

To add an event to the calendar, go to month view, then tap and hold your finger on the day the event or appointment falls on.

In the popup that appears. Tap 'title', then type a name for the appointment or event.

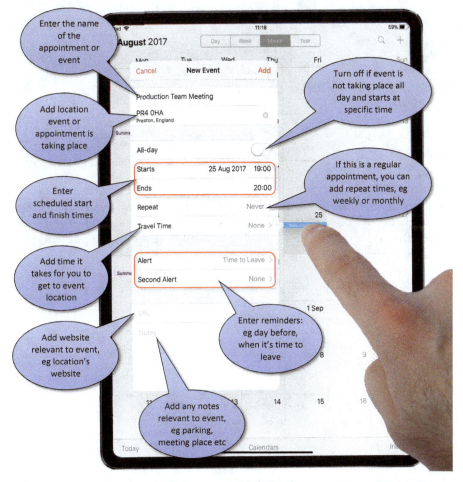

Do the same for location, and select your times. Once you are finished tap done.

Add a Recurring Appointment

To add a recurring event to the calendar, tap and hold your finger on the first day the event falls on.

In the popup that appears. Tap 'title', then type a title (what the event or appointment is).

Do the same for location, and select your times.

Now to create a recurring event, tap 'repeat' in the 'new event' window. Here you can set the event to recur once a week, once a month, every two weeks and so on. All you have to do is tap on the one you want.

You can also set a custom option, tap 'custom'. Say the event occurs every three weeks. Set the frequency to 'weekly'. Then tap 'every' and select the number of weeks. In this example, three weeks, so slide the number to '3'.

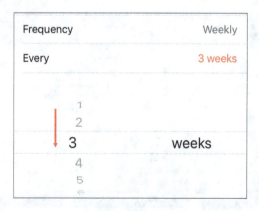

Once you are finished, tap 'repeat' on the top left of the repeat window to go back. Tap 'add' to add the event to your calendar.

Adding an Appointment from a Message

Apple Mail, iMessage and FaceTime will scan your message for phrases that look like dates and times and will create a link in the email for you. To add the event from the email or text message, tap on this link. From the popup box tap 'create event'.

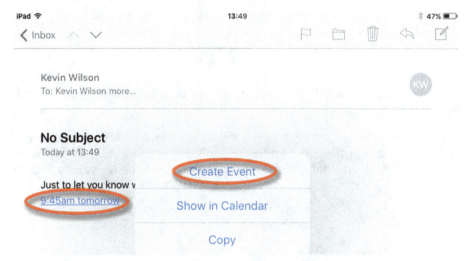

Enter a title and location if calendar didn't pick one up from the email. You can also tweak the information and add additional information if required.

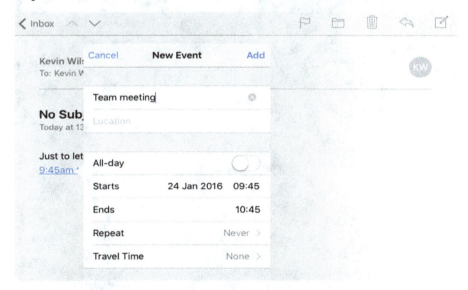

Once you have done that, tap 'add' to enter the appointment into your calendar.

FaceTime

To use FaceTime, tap the icon on the home screen. You will need your Apple ID and a wifi/data connection to the internet.

When you open FaceTime, you will be prompted to sign in if you haven't already done so.

Once FaceTime has opened, you'll see in the main window a preview of your camera. On the left hand side you'll see a darkened panel where you'll find your contacts, history of calls and a search for you to search for people

Making a Call

In this demonstration, Claire is going to FaceTime Sophie from her iPad. Start typing the person's name you want to FaceTime into the search field on the top left of the screen. If the name is in your contacts, then it will appear underneath. Tap the little camera icon next to the name to make a FaceTime call.

Wait for the other person to answer...

Claire's iPad is on the left in the demo below. She is placing a FaceTime call to Sophie who's using the iPad on the right.

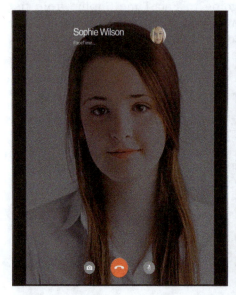

You can see on Sophie's iPad on the right, it's telling her who is calling with the caller id at the top of the screen.

In the background of your screen, you'll see a preview of your camera - so make sure you're squarely in the frame so when the call is answered, the other person can see you clearly.

Along the bottom of the screen you'll see some icons. The red 'decline' button, declines the call. To answer the call just tap the green 'accept' button.

You'll also see two other icons above these two. Tap 'remind me' to set a reminder to call back. If you can't talk, tap 'message' to send a quick message such as 'on my way', 'can I call you later', or 'cant talk now'.

Once the other person answers, you can now have a video conversation. The onboard microphone on your iPhone/iPad will pick up your voice, so just talk naturally.

You'll see an image of the person calling in the centre of your screen with a thumbnail view of your own camera on the top right. Here's the view of Claire's call from her iPad.

Along the bottom, you'll see three icons. If these icons disappear, tap the screen once and they'll re-appear. The icon on the left opens up your effects panel, the middle icon closes the call, and the right hand icon opens up the panel fully.

It's a great tool to keep in touch with family, see the kids if you're away, and so they can see you too.

During your call, tap on the screen to reveal the in call icons

Tap on the three dots icon on the right to reveal the full panel.

On the top row of icons you have a button for adding effects, ending the call, and switching between front and rear camera on your iPad.

On the second row you have buttons to mute your microphone, mute iPad speaker, and blank your camera.

Under these icons you can open an iMessage conversation and see contact details of the person you're face-timing with.

Adding Effects

During a call, you can add all sorts of effects to your image. To do this, tap the effects icon on the bottom left of the in call window.

Select the type of effect you want to add. You can add filters, text, shapes, and icons. In this example we're going to add a text effect.

Tap the text icon, select an effect,

Then type in some text and drag the effect into place.

Lets have a look at what the effect will look like. This is what the other person you're talking to will see.

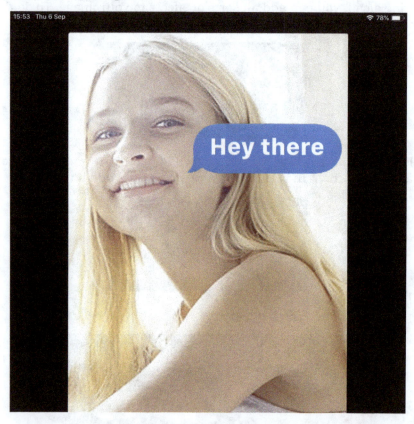

Tap the small x on the top right of the effects panel to close. Tap the effects icon to close the panel.

Try some of the other effects and filters on the panel. Try adding a shape or an icon and see what happens.

Group FaceTime

Group FaceTime allows you to set up groups and chat to up to 32 people at a time. To use Group FaceTime, all participants must have iOS 12 or later, otherwise you won't be able to add them to the group.

To place a group call, on the left hand panel tap on the + icon on the upper corner.

Type the names of the people you want to place a group call to in the 'to' field, or tap the + icon and add them from your contacts list.

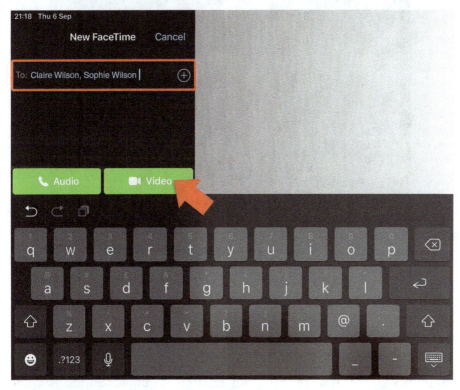

If they all have iOS 12 or later installed on their devices, you'll see two green buttons appear along the bottom of the side panel.

Tap on 'video' to place a group video call.

When your contacts answer, you'll see a thumbnail of each of them on your main display.

In this demo, the girls are having a group FaceTime with grand dad.

You'll see a thumbnail of your own camera in the bottom right of the screen. The other contacts in your group will show up in a thumbnail window in the main area of the screen.

The clever bit is, when one of your contacts starts talking, their thumbnail window will temporarily enlarge. As usual, Sophie is doing all the talking so her thumbnail window is enlarged.

FaceTime is useful for keeping in touch with family and friends who don't live near by, or live in another country.

Adding a Contact

To add a contact, type the person's email address into the search field on the left hand side of the screen and tap on the email address that pops up below.

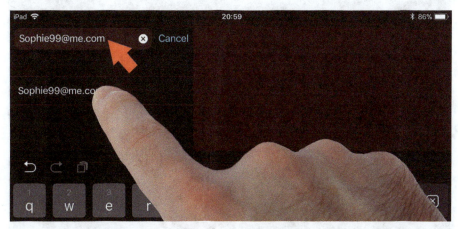

From the selections tap 'add new contact'. This will allow you to enter their name, address, phone numbers and so on.

Enter the person's details into the correct fields.

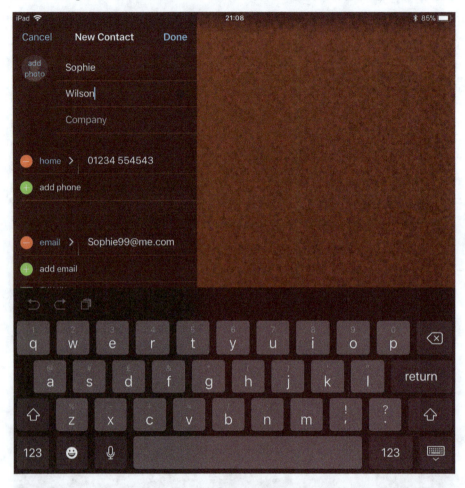

Tap in each field and add the information using the onscreen keyboard. You don't have to fill in every field, just the ones that are relevant.

Tap on 'add photo' on the top left. You can either take a photo using your camera, or select one from your photo library.

Tap 'done' when you're finished.

iMessage

You can send photos and videos and also voice messages to anyone with an Apple device. To start iMessage, tap the icon on the dock on your home screen.

When you open iMessage, you will see a list of all your received messages. Tap on a message to read and reply. Tap the new message icon on the top of the messages list on the left hand pane.

Tap the + sign to add an address or phone number from your contacts.

Type your message in the box indicated with the red arrow.

You can send a voice message by tapping and holding your finger on the mic icon. Record your message, then release your finger to stop.

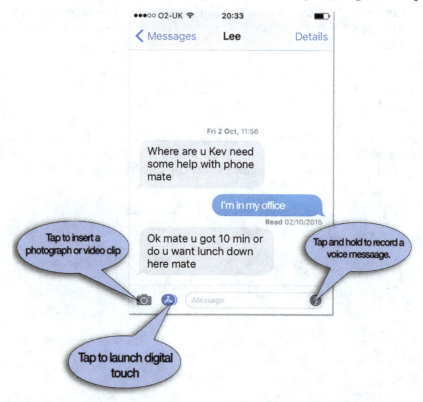

From the options that appear, select from the icons below.

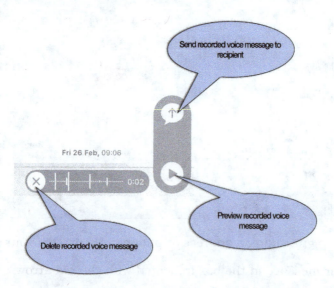

Sending Photos from Photos App

To send a photograph or video you've taken previously, tap the small app icon on the bottom left of your message window.

Tap the 'photos' icon.

Select the photo you want to send from your photos. Tap 'all photos' to see more.

Type in a message where it says 'add comment or send'.

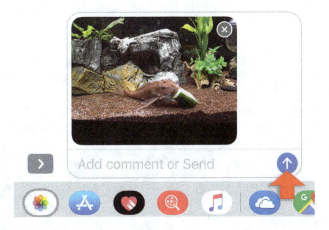

Tap the blue icon on the right hand side to send the image.

Sending Photos from Camera

To send a photograph or video, tap the small camera icon on the bottom left of your message window.

Your camera app will open up. Select 'photo' from the list on the bottom right, then tap on the white circle to take the picture.

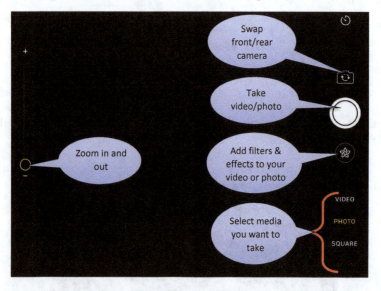

Once you've taken your photo, you can add effects and annotate the image before you send it. Just tap the markup icon on the right hand side of the screen. Tap 'save' on the top right, then tap the blue arrow to send.

Adding Effects

You can also add effects to a photo or video. To do this, select 'photo' from the list on the bottom right, then tap on the white/red circle to take the picture.

Once you've taken your picture, select the effects icon from the panel on the right hand side. Then select an effect from the panel that appears along the bottom.

 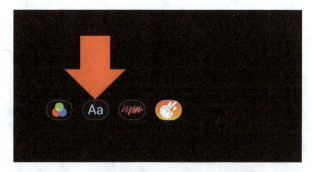

Add some text and effects to your image. Tap and drag the effect into place.

 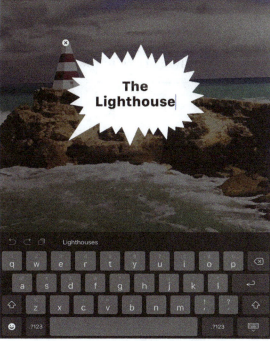

Try a few of the other effects.

Tap the blue arrow on the right hand side to send immediately, or tap 'done' on the top right of the screen to return to the message window.

If you returned to the message window, enter a message in the text field, tap the blue arrow to the right of the text field to send.

Digital Touch in iMessage

In digital touch mode, you can draw with your finger and send animations.

Tap the store icon to the left side of the text field to reveal additional options. Then tap the digital touch icon.

This opens up the digital touch interface. Make sure you select the digital touch icon on the bottom left. Tap the red circle on the left hand side.

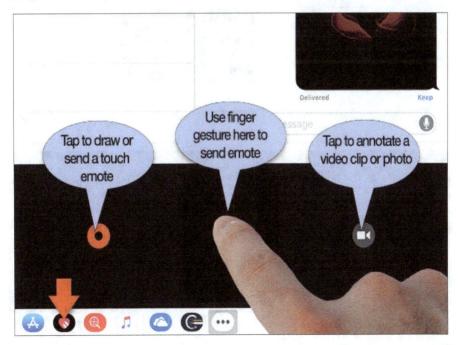

This will allow you to use certain finger gestures to send different emotes. For example, you can use one finger to draw or write something, press with one finger to send a fireball effect, tap with two fingers to send a kiss and so on. Here's a list of a few of the good ones...

You can also draw using your finger, tap on a colour along the left hand side, then draw a diagram on the black screen in the centre. Press on a colour to open up the colour wheel if the colour you want isn't listed.

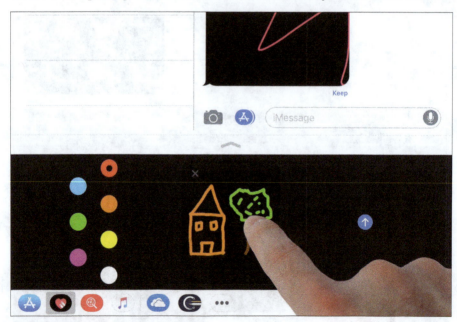

Tap on the blue arrow to the right to send.

You can also annotate a video or photograph using digital touch. To do this, from digital touch interface, tap the camera icon.

Tap the red button to start recording. While the video is recording, use the digital touch tools to draw on it. Tap a colour, then draw or write on the image with your finger.

The white button at the bottom left takes a photo, while the red button in the centre records a video.

Try a few 'tap and holds' with two fingers to add a few hearts. Or tap with two fingers to send a kiss.

Tap the record button again to stop recording. Tap the blue arrow at the bottom right to send your finished piece.

You can also share gifs which are short animations. Select the digital touch icon circled below. Then along the bottom of the screen, select the 'search gif' icon. Tap on a gif to add it to your message or type in to the 'find images' field to search for something specific.

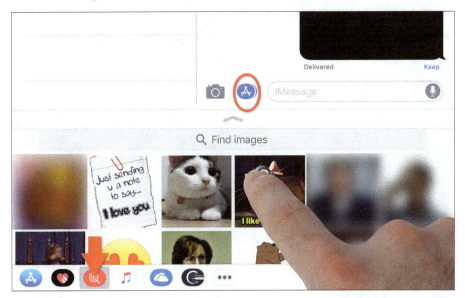

You can also share what music you are listening to on iTunes. Select the digital touch icon circled below. Then along the bottom of the screen, select the 'iTunes' icon.

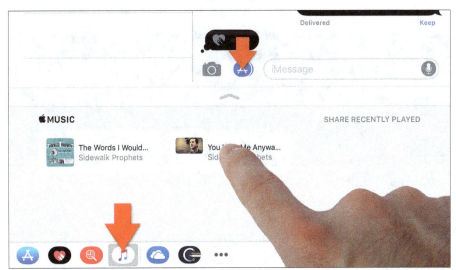

You'll see all the music you have been listening to or currently listening to on your iPad. Tap on a track to share.

Sending Payments with iMessage

You can send payments to contacts on iMessage using Apple Pay. This only works between Apple devices at the moment, so you can't send payments to users of other phones or tablets.

Tap the store icon to the left side of the text field to reveal additional options. Then tap the Apple Pay icon.

If you have Apple Pay set up on your iPad, you'll see this icon at the bottom.

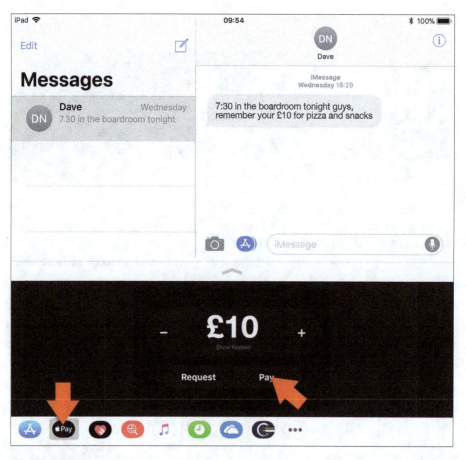

Enter the amount. Either use the + and - buttons to increase/decrease the amount, or tap 'show keypad' to tap in the amount. Once you're done hit 'pay'.

If people are owing you money, you can enter the amount as above and tap 'request' to send them an invite to pay you the amount.

Emojis

Also known as emoticons, emojis are little ideograms used to express emotion in a text based world. These ideograms could be facial expressions such as smilies, common objects, places, and animals. You can use them in iMessage, text messaging, and email.

Using Emojis

You'll find the emoji panel on your on screen keyboard. To open the panel, tap the small 'smiley' icon on the bottom left.

Swipe left to scroll through the list of emojis. You can also tap the grey icons along the bottom to jump to different categories, eg food, places, sports, and so on.

Tap on the emoji you want to insert.

Tap 'abc' on the left hand side to close the emoji panel.

183

AirDrop

AirDrop allows you to transfer files from one device to another using bluetooth wireless technology.

To use AirDrop you will need a compatible device, such as the iPhone 5 or later, fourth-generation iPad, iPad mini, and fifth-generation iPod touch, and have both Bluetooth and Wi-Fi enabled.

Swipe your finger downwards from the top right edge of your screen to open control center. Tap the icons to yurn on Wi-Fi and Bluetooth.

To enable AirDrop open Control Centre and press the AirDrop icon. Make yourself discoverable to just those in your contacts.

Be careful if you select 'everyone' as this means anyone in your vicinity that has an airdrop enabled device can connect to and send files to your device, which could be a possible security risk.

To Send a file to Someone using AirDrop

You can send a file or photo from your iPad to another iPhone or iPad.

In this example, I am going to send a photo. So launch Photos app.

Tap the image or video you want to share from your albums, tap next.

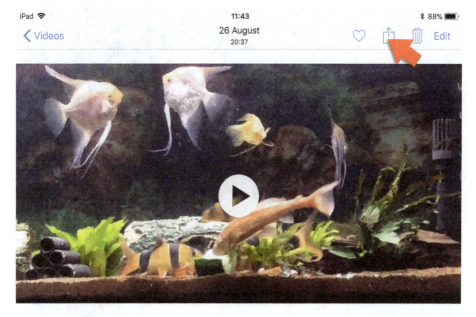

Tap on the Share icon. AirDrop will detect other devices in the vicinity. In this example, AirDrop has detected my iPhone. This is the one I want to share with.

Tap the icon of the person/device you want to send to.

Now when you send the photo, the other person will get a prompt to download the image. Accept the confirmation and your image will download.

The image/video will be added to your photo library. The photo sent has appeared in photos app on the iPhone.

This works the same for other files too, just select the file and tap the share icon. Files will appear in the relevant apps; music will go to iTunes and files will be stored in Files app. If iOS doesn't recognise the file type, then it will ask you what app you want to open the file with.

To Receive a File from Someone using AirDrop

Make sure your AirDrop is enabled on your device.

AirDrop will try to negotiate the connection with near by devices.

More often than not, the file will automatically download. If you get a prompt, tap on Accept when the photo comes through

Go into your photos app and the photo will be stored in there.

Chapter 5

Using Multimedia

Your iPad is a multimedia rich device, meaning you can take photos and record videos. You can even edit and enhance your photos, correct colour and brightness.

You can post your photographs to your favourite social media account for the world to see.

You can create slide shows, edit your videos, download and watch TV programmes and films.

You can download and play any kind of music you can think of, all from your iPad.

So lets begin by taking a look at the Photos App. Take a look at the video resources

www.elluminetpress.com/ipad-pro-mm

Photos

Using the photos app, you can import photos from a memory card or digital camera, edit and share photos taken with the on board cameras on your iPad.

Import Photos

There are two adapters available to accomplish this: the Lightning to SD Card Reader, or the Lightning to USB Adapter.

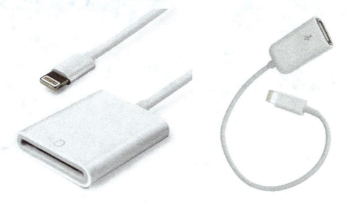

The card reader enables you to insert the SD card from your camera and copy images from it.

The card reader plugs into the docking port on the bottom of the iPad. Launch the iPhoto app. Tap on camera or card.

Chapter 5: Using Multimedia

You can also connect your camera directly using a lightning to USB connector. Plug the connector into the bottom of your iPad, then plug the USB cable that came with your camera into the other end of the lightning to USB adapter.

When iPad detects your media, it will prompt you with an import screen. Tap the photographs you want to import and then tap import to copy the photos across.

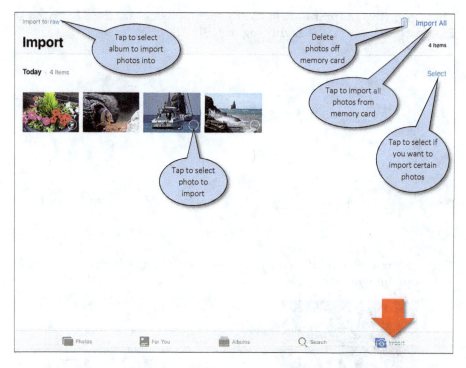

Once the photos have been imported, you will see a prompt asking you whether to keep the images or delete them.

If you select keep, this leaves all the photos intact on the memory card. If you select delete, this deletes the photos you just imported off the memory card.

Once all the photos have been imported it is safe to delete the photos off the card.

190

Browsing Through your Photos

Along the bottom of the photos app you can view your all your photos together, selected memories, albums, and search for photos. You can view your photos by year, month or day so you can find things easily.

Scroll up and down to scroll through photographs and videos you have taken.

Tap on a photo to view it in full.

Editing Photos

You can do some basic editing on your iPad. You can lighten up dark images, crop and rotate your photos.

To do this, select 'photos' from the panel along the bottom of the screen, then tap on the photo you want to adjust.

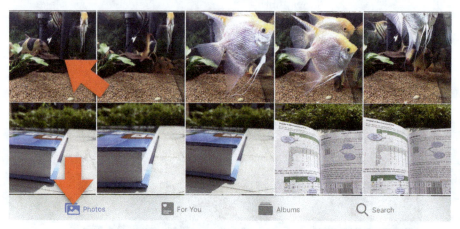

When your photo opens up, tap 'edit' on the top right of the screen.

When the adjustment screen appears, you'll see three icons on the left hand side. On the right, you'll see some adjustment dials.

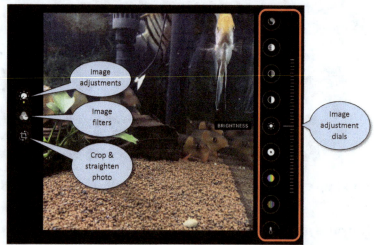

Adjusting Images

To adjust images, tap the image adjustment icon from the three on the left hand side. The image adjustment dials will appear down the right hand side. Let's take a look at what each icon does.

- Auto
- Exposure
- Brilliance
- Highlights (bright or white parts of image)
- Shadows (dark or black parts of image)
- Contrast
- Brightness
- Black Point (brightness of the black parts of image)
- Color saturation (intensity of the colors)
- Color vibrance
- Warmth (white balance - bluish or orange tint to photo)
- Tint
- Sharpness
- Photo definition
- Noise reduction (removes noise from photo)

To adjust the image, select one of the tools on the panel. For example, to brighten up the whole image, select brightness. You can drag the panel upwards with your finger to see all the icons. Tap the icon you want, then drag the dial up or down to adjust.

Select another icon to adjust, or tap 'done' on the top right when you're finished.

Crop an Image

To crop an image, tap the 'crop and rotate' icon from the three on the left hand side. The image crop dials will appear down the right hand side.

Around the edges of your image you'll see some crop handles. Tap and drag these around the part of the image you want to keep.

You can also use the two lower icons on the right hand side to remove distortion from your image.

Tap and drag the dial up and down to adjust the image.

Rotate an Image

To rotate an image, tap the 'crop and rotate' icon from the three on the left hand side.

Tap the rotate icon on the right hand side.

Tap and drag the dial up and down to rotate the image.

Tap 'done' on the top right when you're finished.

Creating Albums

You can create albums to organise your photos. To do this, tap 'photos' on the bottom left of your screen.

Tap 'select' on the top right

Tap the photos you want to add to your album.

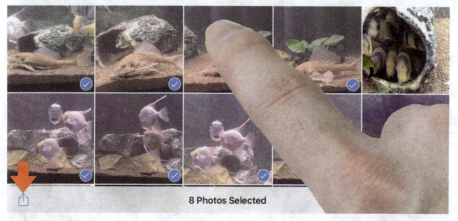

Tap the share icon on the bottom left.

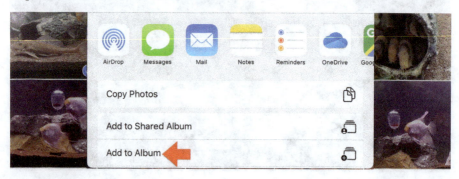

Scroll down, select 'add to album'

Now if you want to create a new album, tap 'new album' and type in a name. If you want to add the photos to an existing album, tap the name of the album under 'my albums'.

You'll find your albums in the 'albums' section of your photos app

Search for Photos

The photos app automatically scans your photos for recognisable objects, animals, places and people. To search, tap 'search' on the bottom right of your screen.

Type in your keywords in the search field at the top of the screen.

Sharing Photos

To share a photo with a friend, or on social media, first tap 'photos' on the bottom left.

Select the photo you want to share.

Once the photo opens up, tap the share icon in the top right corner.

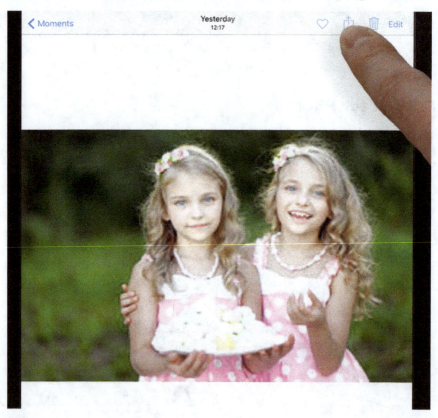

Select the app you want to use to share your photo. You can share the photo via email, messages, or social media.

For example, select 'Facebook' from the list of icons to post on Facebook.

Type a message in your post, then hit 'post'.

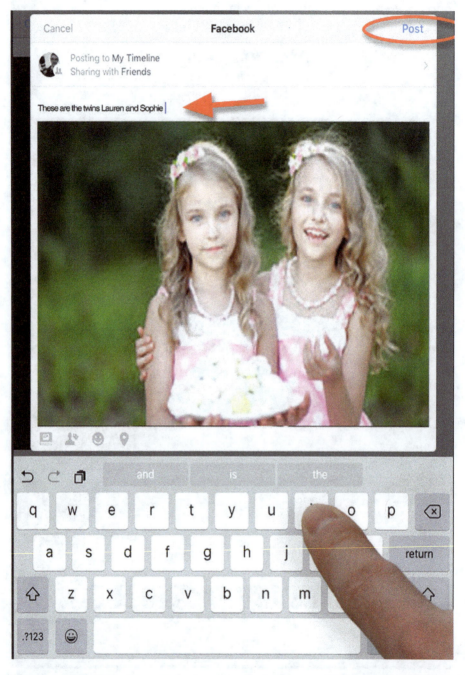

You can use the same procedure for Twitter, email, iMessage and any other social media you use. Just select the icon from the icons list

Camera App

Tap the camera icon on the home screen.

You can use your iPad as a camera to take photos and record video.

Along the right side of your screen you have some icons. At the top you can turn on/off live photos, add a timer, turn on/off flash, and switch between forward/rear cameras.

The white circle takes the photo, the thumbnail icon underneath shows you the last photo taken. Underneath this you can select the type of video or photo you want to take: time lapse, slow motion, video, photo, portrait, square photo and panoramic photo. Swipe your finger up and down over these to select.

You can adjust the zoom using the slider on the left hand side of the image. Drag the circle on the bar upwards to zoom in, and downwards to zoom out.

If you're having trouble focusing, tap and hold your finger on the object you want to focus on. This will lock the exposure and focus on that object, so it doesn't change, making it easier to take the photo.

Tap the white circle on the right hand side as normal to take the photo.

You can also adjust the brightness before you take a photo. To do this tap on the screen and you'll see a yellow square show up with a vertical line with a slider on it.

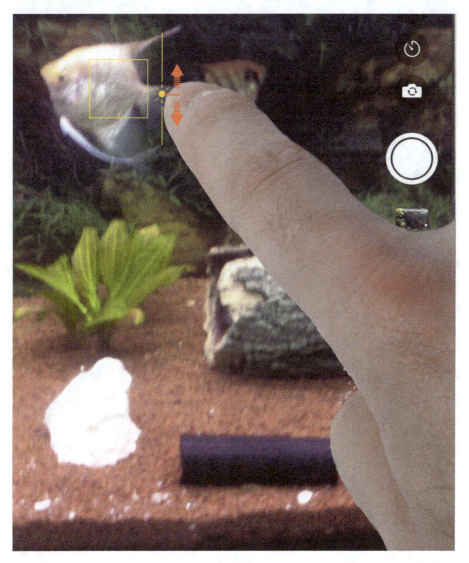

Drag the slider upward to brighten up the image, slide it downward to darken the image.

Tap the white circle to take the photo as normal.

Take a look at the 'taking photos' video demo in the 'multimedia' section of the accompanying resources. Scan code or go to following website.

www.elluminetpress.com/ipad-pro-mm

Adjusting your Photo

Once you have taken your photo, you can adjust, enhance, crop, or rotate the image.

To do this, tap the photo icon on the right hand side of the screen under the white shutter button.

This will open the photo up on the edit screen.

From here you can adjust, enhance, crop, rotate and share the image. See "Adjusting Images" on page 193 topage 195.

Panoramic Photos

Panoramic shots are great for scenery and landscapes. Photos app allows you to automatically take a series of photos and it stitches them together into a long panoramic image.

To take panoramic photos, open your camera app, select pano from the right hand side of the screen. You might need to scroll down the selections if it isn't visible.

Now, move your iPad to the start of the scene and tap the white circle. You'll notice in the centre of the screen a rectangular box, this will start to fill as you move your iPad across the scene. In this demonstration, I'm taking a panoramic photo of a mountain range.

Position your iPad camera at the beginning of the mountain range on the left, tap the white 'take photo' icon on the right of your screen. Now move your camera along the mountain range until you get to the end. You'll see the rectangular box in the centre of the screen fill up as you do so. Tap the white circle again to finish. Make sure you stand in one spot, the panoramic photos don't work if you walk along with it.

Recording Video

You can record video using the camera app. Select 'video' from the list on the bottom right of your screen.

To take the best looking video, use your iPad in a horizontal orientation as shown below.

Tap the red circle icon on the right hand side of the screen to start recording. Tap on any part of the screen to focus on that point during the video. Use the slider on the left hand side to zoom in and out. Tap the red circle icon on the right hand side to stop recording.

Take a look at the 'recording video' demo in the 'multimedia' section of the accompanying resources.

www.elluminetpress.com/ipad-pro-mm

Enhancing Video

You can use many of the same adjustments, filters as well as crop, and rotate on your videos. Video editing supports all video formats captured on iPad.

To edit a video, select 'photos' from the panel along the bottom of the screen, then tap on the video clip you want to adjust. Videos have a clip length indicator on the bottom right of the thumbnail.

When your video opens up, tap 'edit' on the top right of the screen.

On the left, tap the adjustment icon.

When the adjustment screen appears, you'll see three icons on the left hand side. On the right, you'll see some adjustment dials. These are the same as for photos, see "Adjusting Images" on page 193

Music App

To start the music app, tap the icon on your dock.

Once music app has loaded you can see all the albums that are currently on your iPad

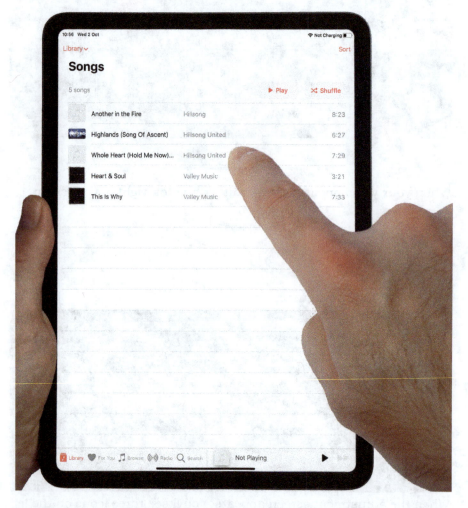

Tapping on the album cover brings up the song list. Just tap the song on the song list and it will start playing. Time to put on your headphones.

There are two ways you can buy your music. You can subscribe to Apple Music and stream any track you like from the music library for a monthly subscription fee. Or you can purchase and download the albums or tracks individually from the iTunes Store (see page 221).

Apple Music

Let's take a look at Apple Music. With Apple Music you need a constant internet connection. At the time of writing, there are three subscription options for Apple Music.

- £4.99 a month gives you full access to the music library and is only available for University/College students.

- £9.99 a month gets you full access to the music library and many radio stations available. This is an individual account and allows only one account access to the iTunes Store.

- £14.99 a month gets you full access to the music library and radio stations and allows up to 6 people to sign in and listen to their music. This is ideal for families.

To sign up, open the Music App and from the list of icons along the bottom of the screen, select 'for you'.

To get started, tap 'choose a plan'.

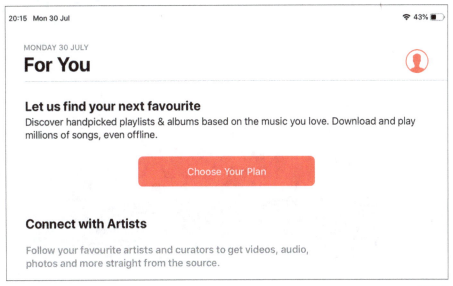

Chapter 5: Using Multimedia

Choose a membership programme, then tap 'join apple music'.

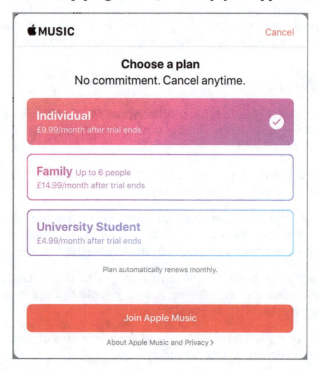

Enter your Apple ID username and password, or confirm with touch ID, if you have this enabled, by placing your finger on the home button.

Tap the genres you like. Tap 'next' when you're done.

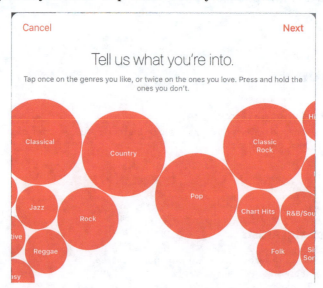

The Main Screen

You can use the icons along the bottom of Apple Music to navigate around.

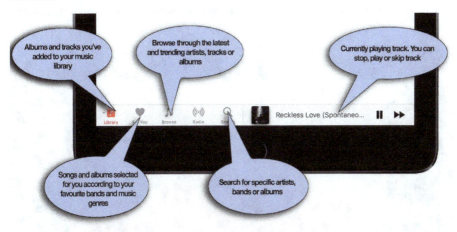

Tap the currently playing track to reveal the album or track details

Searching for Music

Select the artists you like. If you don't see all the ones you like, tap 'more artists' on the bottom left. If the artist you're looking for isn't there, you can add them. To do this tap 'add an artist' and enter their name.

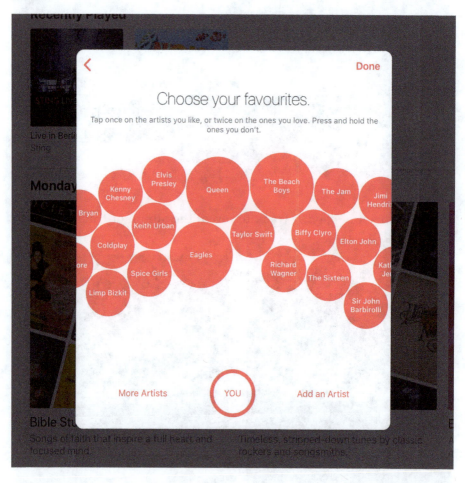

Now, you can search for any artist, band or song you can think of. To do this, on Apple iTunes Music's home screen, select 'search' from the icons along the bottom of the screen.

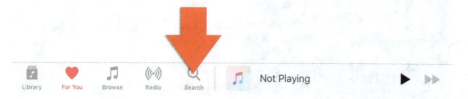

Type an artist's/album name into the search field at the top.

Select the closest match from the list of suggestions.

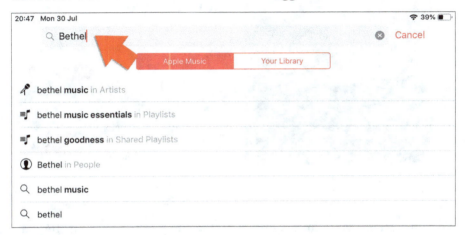

From here you can tap on a song to listen to it, open an album, add to your music library, or you can build your own playlists.

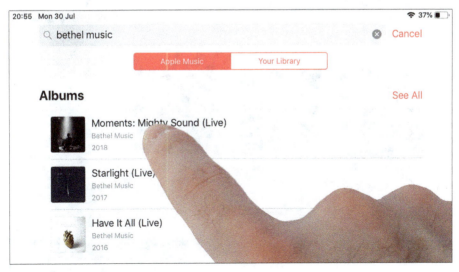

Tap on an album to open it.

Add to Library

You can start to create a library of your favourite music, so it's easy to find. To do this, tap the + sign next to the song you want to add to your library. If you want to add the whole album tap '+add'.

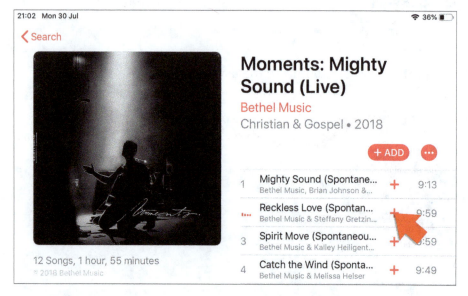

You can access your music library using the 'library' icon on the bar along the bottom of the screen.

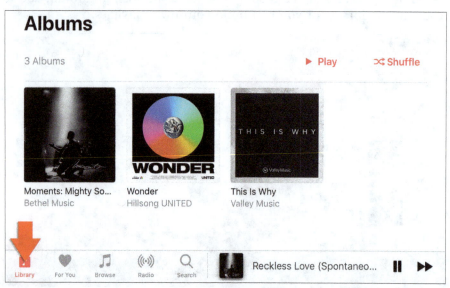

Tap an album to open it, tap on a track to play it.

Creating Playlists

You can create playlists to play all your favourite tracks from any album or artist.

To add a track to a playlist, tap and hold your finger on the track in your list of songs, then from the popup menu, select 'add to a playlist.

Select the playlist you want to add the track to, if it exists. Or tap 'new playlist' to add the track to a new playlist.

You'll find your playlists in your library. Tap 'library' on the bottom left. Tap the menu on the top left, select 'playlists'.

Importing CDs

Somewhat outdated technology nowadays, but if you still have audio CDs, you can import them. First you'll need an external CD drive. Plug the drive into a USB port on your Mac and insert a CD.

Open the music app on your Mac, your CD will appear under 'devices' on the left hand panel. Click on the CD to open. Click 'import CD' to begin.

Click 'ok' on the 'import settings' popup.

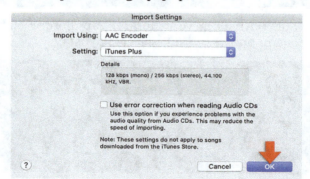

Now to add your imported CD to your iPad. Unplug the external CD player, and plug in your iPad using the USB cable.

Open the finder app and move the window to the right hand side, select your iPad under the 'locations' section on the side panel.

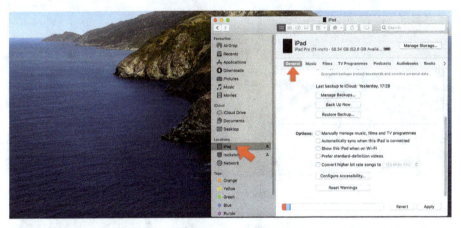

Make sure you select 'general' to display the general settings. Open your music app, move the window to the top left.

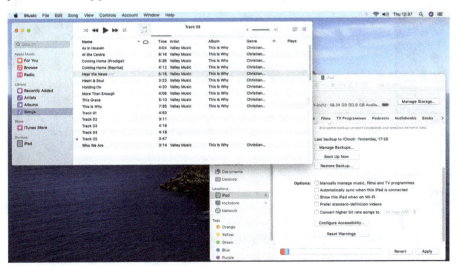

Chapter 5: Using Multimedia

In the music app, the tracks from the CD you just imported will appear on the 'songs' list under the 'library' section on the left hand panel. Select the tracks you want. To do this hold down the command key then click the tracks you want.

Click and drag the selected tracks to the finder window on the bottom right of the screen.

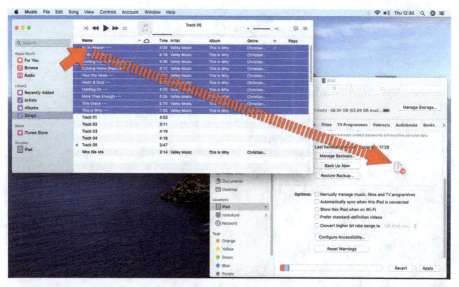

You'll be able to find the tracks on your iPad.

Podcasts App

You can listen to all sorts of podcasts. To begin, tap the podcasts icon on your home screen.

Once the app starts, you can browse through the latest podcasts. Along the bottom of the screen you'll see a panel.

The best way to find your podcasts is to search for them. You can search for artist name, program name, or any area of interest. To search, tap the search icon on the panel along the bottom of the screen.

219

Type the podcast you're looking for in the search field at the top of the screen, the select the podcast you want from the results.

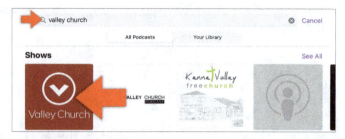

Tap 'subscribe' to get updates when new episodes are posted.

You'll find all your subscribed podcasts in your library or on the 'listen now' tab.

Tap 'recently added' on the left hand side. Tap the podcast icon to open the episodes.

Tap the play icon to continue listening, or tap 'all episodes' to see all available episodes for that particular podcast.

iTunes Store

To access the iTunes Store, tap the 'iTunes Store' icon on your home screen.

Once the app has loaded you can browse through music, movies and tv shows - tap the category icons across the top of the screen. You can also type what you are looking for in the search field on the top right of the screen.

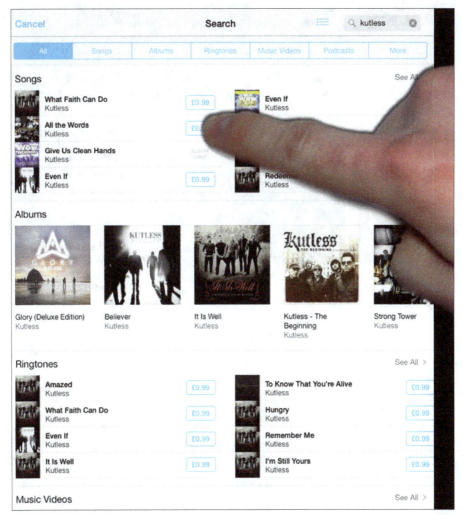

Music

Within the music section of the iTunes Store, you can browse through the latest releases, charts and different genres.

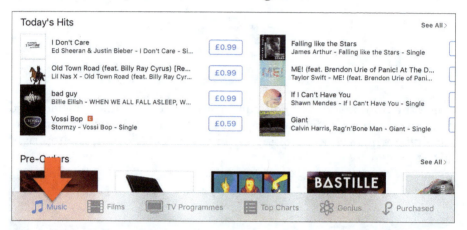

To search for your favourite tracks, artists and albums, type your search into the field at the top. Then select the closest match from the suggestions.

Along the top of the search results, you can view by song or album. Scroll up and down the list to see the songs and albums.

Tap on the price tag to download the song. Once the songs are downloaded you will find then in your recently added playlist.

Films & TV

You can stream films and TV programmes directly to your iPad from the iTunes Store. You can buy or rent what you want to watch. To to this, select 'films' or 'tv programmes' from the panel along the bottom of the screen.

You can also search for a specific title using the search field at the top right of the screen, or to browse your favourite genre, tap 'genres' on the top left.

Search for a film or TV programme you want to watch either by typing the title into the search or browse through the genres. Tap on the thumbnail cover to view the details.

On the film details screen you'll be able to read details about the film, reviews and ratings. Tap 'rent' or 'buy'. Verify your purchase using the Touch ID, or your Apple ID username and password.

You'll find your downloaded films and TV programmes in the library section of the TV App.

Apple TV App

Gearing up for Apple's new streaming service Apple TV+, the Apple TV App becomes your entertainment hub where you'll find all your purchased or rented films, music, and TV programmes. You'll find the app on your home screen.

Here, you'll be able to subscribe to Apple's streaming service and stream the latest TV Programmes and movies direct to your iPad.

Watch Now

When you first start the app, you'll land on the 'watch now' page.

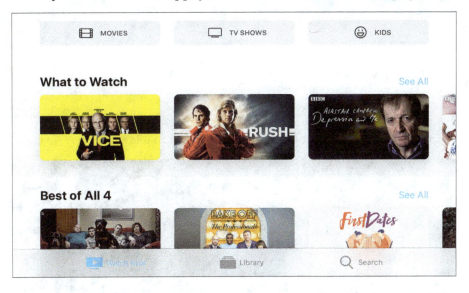

Along the top of the screen you can select movies, tv shows or kids shows.

Along the bottom of the screen you can browse with 'watch now', see your library of media you've purchased or rented, or search for a particular artists, actor, or title.

In the middle of the screen, you'll be able to scroll through current TV Shows and movie releases. Tap on the thumbnail icons to view details, or tap 'see more' on the top right to see more content.

Library

Select 'library' from the panel along the bottom of the screen.

Select 'movies' to see movies you've rented or purchased, similarly select 'tv shows' if you've downloaded a tv show.

Tap on the film or tv programme to begin playback.

Airplay

Airplay allows wireless streaming of audio and video data to an Apple TV or compatible receiver on your TV.

For this to work, both your iPad and Apple TV will need to be on the same WiFi network. This is usually the case in most homes.

To mirror your iPad, swipe downwards from the top right edge of your screen to open your control centre.

Tap on 'screen mirroring' or 'airplay mirroring' and select your Apple TV from the list. Enter your passcode if prompted.

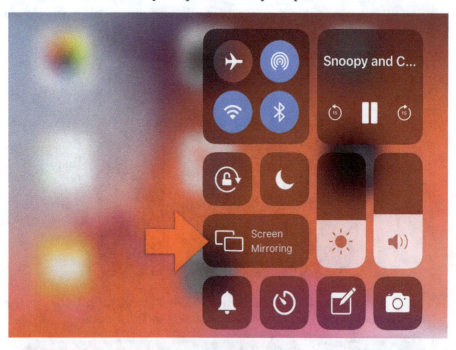

If you don't know the Apple TV passcode, go on your Apple TV, then go to settings > Airplay, select 'Onscreen code'.

You can turn off the code or set a new one.

Apple Pencil

Apple Pencil is sold separately from the iPad, so you'll need to buy one from the Apple store. Note that the new iPad Pros do not support the first generation pencil, so when buying, make sure you order the second generation apple pencil.

Apple Pencil is a stylus you can use to draw directly onto the iPad's main screen within a variety of different apps.

You can use your pencil in Notes, Pages, Keynote, Microsoft Word, Excel and PowerPoint to add drawings, annotations and handwritten notes.

There are also some artistic apps where you can apply pressure to create darker lines or tilt your pencil to shade in areas.

Just type 'apple pencil' into the search field in the app store and you'll find plenty of apps.

Take a look at the apple pencil video demos in the multimedia section of the resources. Scan code or go to following website.

www.elluminetpress.com/ipad-pro-mm

Pair Apple Pencil

The pairing process is fairly straight forward with the new apple pencils.

To pair your pencil, attach it to the side of your iPad. The pencil will clip to the magnetic connector.

When you clip your pencil to the side of your iPad for the first time, you'll get a prompt asking you to connect your pencil. Tap 'connect'.

If your pencil won't pair, make sure your bluetooth is enabled.

Go to Settings > Bluetooth to check.

You may also need to allow your pencil to charge, it won't pair if the battery power is low.

Charge your Pencil (2nd Gen)

Your pencil will also charge while it is on the magnetic connector, so you wont need to connect it to the docking port, or to the power adapter as with the first gen pencil.

Using Apple Pencil

You can use apple pencil to take hand written notes. Open up the notes app.

Along the bottom right of the screen you'll see three icons. Tap the markup icon on the far right. Also swipe up from bottom edge.

You can write directly onto the surface of your iPad.

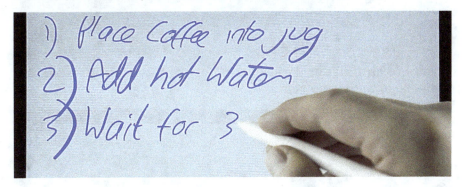

Use the icons on the markup toolbar to select a pen type: marker, highlighter, pencil, eraser and selection/lasso tool, as well as a colour and thickness and opacity (how dark or light the pen is). Tap on a pen type to select, from the popup options, select pen thickness and opacity.

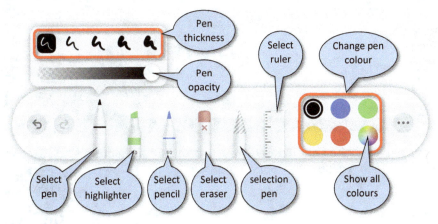

Chapter 5: Using Multimedia

You can highlight and annotate using your favourite productivity apps. In Microsoft Word, select the 'draw' ribbon, select a pen and draw directly onto the document. In Pages, you can draw directly onto the iPad screen on an open document with your pencil - the markup toolbar will appear along the bottom of the screen.

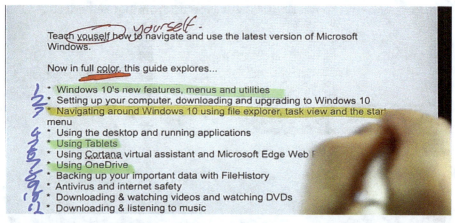

If you are an artist or designer, try out the **Concepts Drawing App** available from the app store.

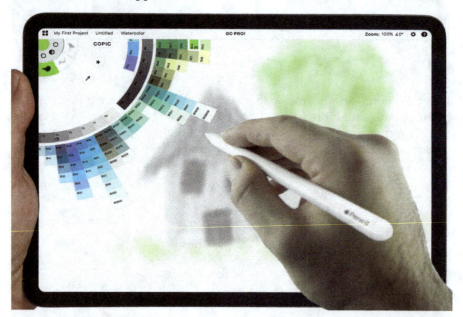

Have a look at the pencil demos in the multimedia section of the video resources. Scan code or go to following website.

www.elluminetpress.com/ipad-pro-mm

Document Scanner

Within the Notes App, you can scan documents and convert them. From the Notes App, tap the camera icon on the bottom right of your screen, or on the top right of the on-screen keyboard.

Tap 'manual' on the right hand side, this is so you can take a photo of each of your pages and gives you more control than auto mode.

Line up the document in the window as shown below, make sure the yellow box covers the whole document.

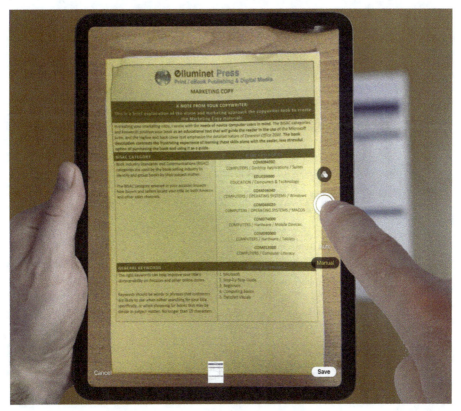

Chapter 5: Using Multimedia

Tap the white button on the right hand side to 'scan the document'. If you have more pages, repeat the process and 'scan' them as well using the white button on the right hand side. Once you have 'scanned' all your pages, tap 'save' on the bottom right corner.

The pages will be added to your note. Tap on the thumbnail to open it up full screen.

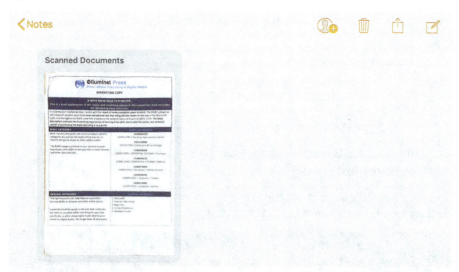

Now you can send the document via email, save it as a PDF, print it or write directly onto the scan with markup.

Tap the 'share' icon on the top right of your screen.

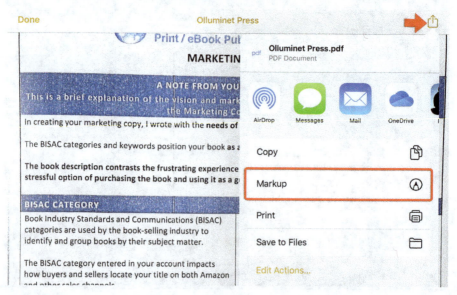

In this demonstration, I'm going to add some annotations with the markup tool. So tap 'markup'.

Select a pen or highlighter from the selection at the bottom left, and select a colour from the bottom right.

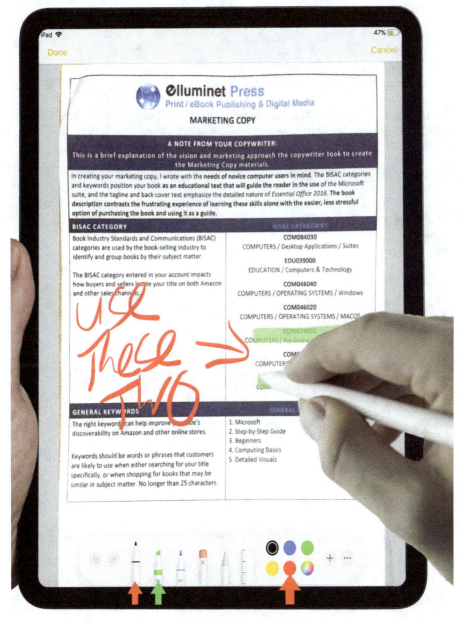

Use your finger or pen to draw directly onto the scanned document. When you're done, tap 'done' on the top left.

Now to send it or save it, tap the 'share' icon on the top right of the screen.

From the drop down, tap 'mail' to email it to someone or 'message' to send via iMessage. From here you can also save it to a PDF or print it if you have air print installed. In this example I'm emailing it.

Enter the email address of the person, add a subject and a message. Tap the send icon to send your message.

QR Code Scanner

A QR code (or quick response code) is a 2D bar code used to provide easy access to information through your iPad. This could be a link to a website. These codes are usually printed on signs, flyers, and other printed material.

To scan a QR code, open your camera app, point it at a QR code, tap the code on the screen to focus.

When the camera reads the code, you'll see a prompt at the top of the screen. Tap to open the link.

Chapter 6

Common Apps

You can pretty much get an app for virtually anything, and these are all available from the app store. Some are free and others you have to buy.

There are games, productivity apps and apps just for fun.

Your iPad comes with some apps built in. You can also download millions more from the App Store.

Lets start by taking a look at the App Store in more detail.

The App Store has had a make over in this version of iOS and has a much easier to use interface Take a look at the video demos

www.elluminetpress.com/using-iPad-pro

App Store

The app store has over 1 million apps available for download direct to your iPad without even going on a computer. To start app store, click App Store app on your main screen.

Once on the app store's main screen, tap the icon on the top right to sign in with your Apple ID if you haven't already done so. If you are already signed in, your Apple ID will be displayed here, you won't need to sign in again.

In the box that appears, enter your Apple ID details.

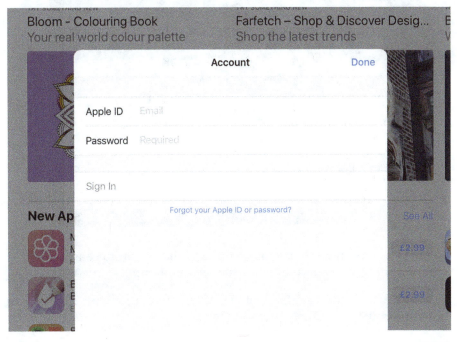

Chapter 6: Common Apps

On the app store, you will find everything from games and entertainment to productivity tools such as word processing, drawing and photo apps.

These are split into games and app sections and you'll find these on the bar along the bottom of the screen.

Also along the bottom you'll find updates to your installed apps, it's worth checking this from time to time, as apps are updated all the time.

The last icon on the bar along the bottom allows you to search the app store for a specific app name or type/genre of app.

You can even find apps for recipes, travel details, maps. There is an app for almost anything you can think of.

Search for Apps

To find an app, tap on 'search' on the bar at the bottom of your screen. Type into the search field on the main screen, as shown below. In this example, I'm going to search for one of my favourite games called 'worms'.

From the suggestions, tap on the closest match. Tap on the image to view more details about the app; here you'll see reviews, price, screen shots and other info.

To download the app, tap 'get' next to the app if it's free, or tap the price tag if it's paid.

If it's a paid app, tap 'purchase' to confirm.

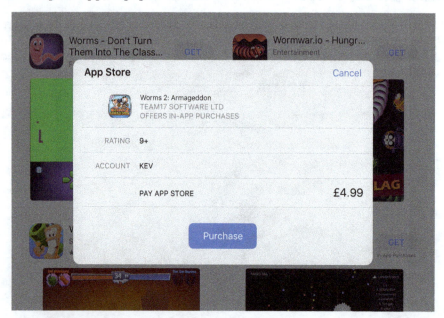

Authorise the purchase with your Apple ID password or if you have touch ID setup, with your thumb print.

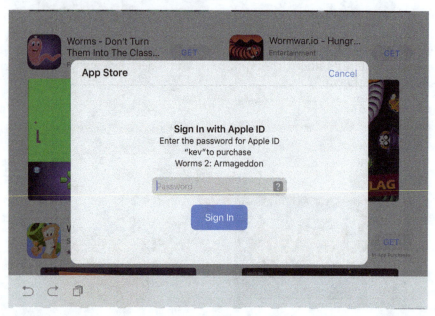

The app will appear on your home screen once it has downloaded and installed itself.

Browsing the Store

If you are more the browsing type, app store has grouped all the apps into categories according to their use. Select 'apps' from the bar on the bottom of the screen. Here you'll see some of the most popular apps, new apps and top selling apps. You can tap on any of these apps to view or download.

Tap on the app's image to view more details, Tap 'see all' at the top of each section to see all the apps in that section. Tap on 'get' or the price to download the app. Scroll down the page to see all the apps in the sections.

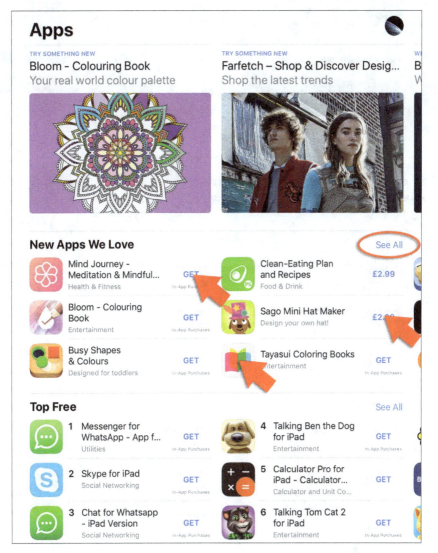

If you scroll down a bit, you'll see a section called 'top categories'.

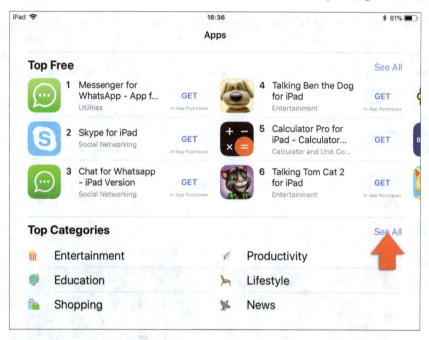

Tap on a category to browse the available apps. In this example, I'm going to explore the 'reference' category.

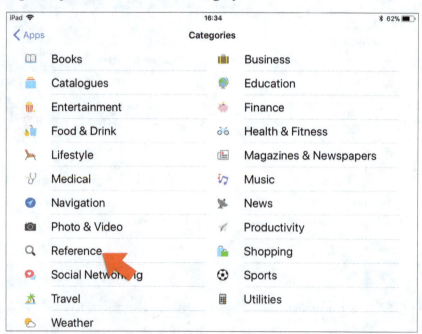

Here, you'll see a list of all the apps available for that category. Again, tap 'see all' on the top right to see the full lists in the different sections.

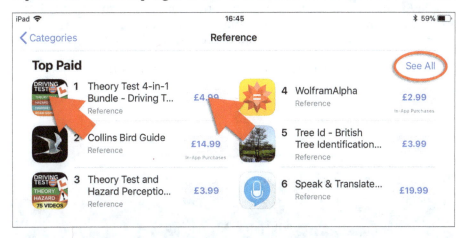

Claire is 18 and learning to drive, so two apps might be of use to her: Theory Test and Hazard Perception. Tap on the apps icon to view more details about the app

Tap the price tag to download and install the app on your iPad

This gives you information about what the app does, what it costs, some screen shots of the app in action and the device requirements in order to run the app.

To purchase an app, just tap on the price tag.

Chapter 6: Common Apps

The Arcade

Apple Arcade is a subscription service that allows you to play the latest arcade games. At the time of writing you can take out a free trial for a month, then it costs £4.99 a month to continue using the service.

To activate the service, tap 'arcade' on the panel along the bottom of the screen,

Tap 'try it free'. The confirm your purchase using touch id

You can browse through the games on the main page. Scroll down to the bottom of the page to see different categories of games you can play. Tap a category to select.

Tap on the game icon to see more information...

Tap 'get' to download the game, tap 'play' to start the game.

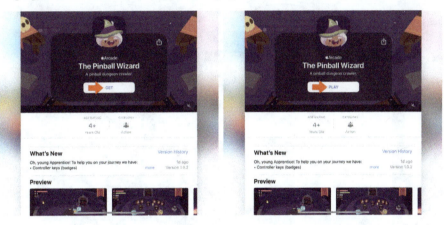

You'll find all your downloaded games on your home screen.

Taking Notes

To start notes app, tap on the icon on the home screen.

When notes has loaded, you can view your saved notes along the left hand side. Along the top right, you have icons to invite people to collaborate on your note, delete current note, share note, and create a new blank note.

Along the bottom right, you can add check/tick boxes to notes which are good for 'to-do' lists. With the next icon across, you can scan documents, take photos or videos and add them to your note. With the last icon, you can use Apple Pencil to annotate your current note and take hand written notes.

Typing Notes

You can type your notes in as if it were a notepad, using the on screen keyboard.

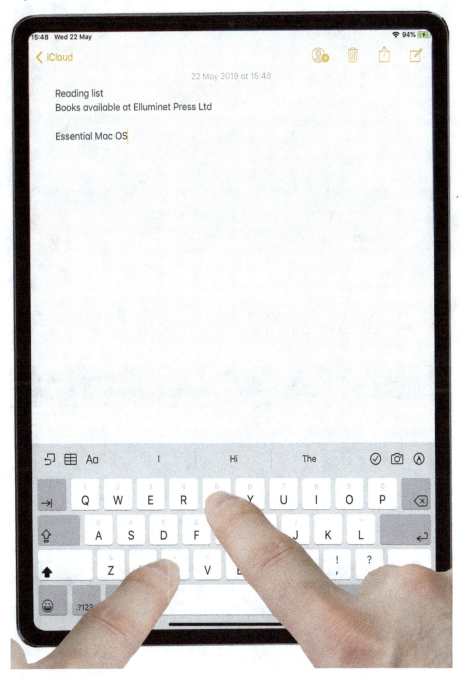

Inserting Photos

You can insert a photograph or video directly into your note. To do this, open a new note, then tap the small + icon on the top right of the on-screen keyboard.

Point your camera at the object you want to take the photograph of. Tap 'use photo' on the bottom right. Tap 'retake' if you want to take the photo again.

Your photo will appear in your notes.

Handwritten Notes

You can use your Apple Pencil to handwrite notes, draw diagrams, and annotate photos. To do this, open a new note, then tap the small pen icon on the top right of the on-screen keyboard.

Your drawing tools will appear along the bottom of the screen. Here, you can choose from a marker pen, highlighter, pencil, eraser, or a lasso tool, as well as your colour pallet.

Tap on the pens to select. When you tap on a pen, you'll see a popup menu. Here, you can select pen thickness and opacity. If the pop up menu doesn't show, tap twice on the pen.

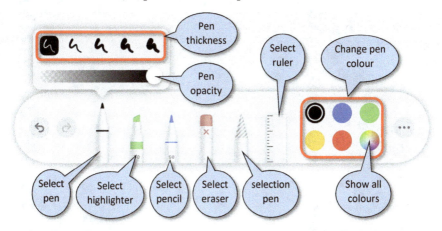

You can also use the selection pen to draw around an object to select it. This helps with copy and paste. There is also an on screen ruler that allows you to draw straight lines with your pen. On the right of the drawing tools you can choose a colour, tap the 'all colours' icon to choose show all colours.

Dictating Notes

Instead of typing, you can dictate notes using the voice dictation feature. To do this, tap the mic icon on the keyboard.

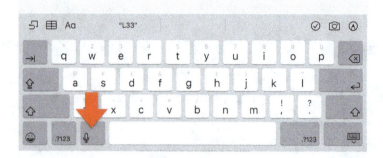

Record your notes using the voice recognition.

Tap done at the bottom, when you are finished.

Organising your Notes

You can create folders to organise your notes. To put a note into a folder, first open the note, then tap the share icon on the top right of the screen. From the drop down, tap 'move to folder'

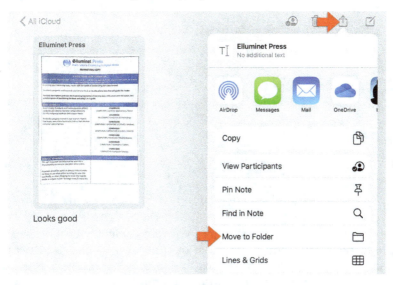

If the folder you want to add the note to exists, select it from the list. If the folder doesn't exist, tap 'new folder'.

Swipe from the left edge of your screen to reveal the folders panel. Tap 'folders' on the top right, if you don't see your folders list.

Chapter 6: Common Apps

Inviting other Users

You can invite other users to view and edit your notes. This can be useful in a meeting where people can add notes from their own iPad. To share a note, tap the invitation icon on the top right hand side of the screen.

Select 'share options'. From here, you can select whether you want people to be able to edit your note, or just view it. Tap 'add people' at the top of the drop down to return to the previous screen. Now, select how you want to send the invitation eg email.

Enter the person's iCloud email address or number (or you can select from your contacts). You can also send via iMessage.

When the other person checks their messages, they will find an email with a link they can click on, which will open the note in the notes app.

You can see in the demo below, the handwritten text at the top is from my iPad, and the typed text at the bottom is from Claire's iPad, who the note was shared with.

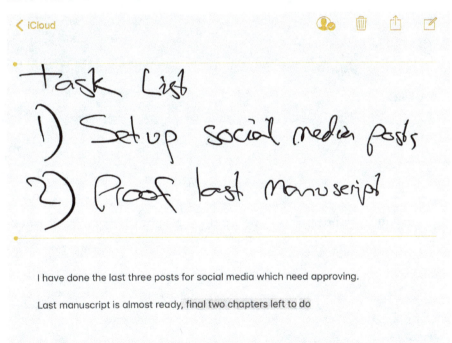

Reminders

With reminders, you can create to do lists, and set alerts to remind you do to certain things.

To start reminders app, tap the icon on the home screen

Create a Reminder

Tap the list you want to add the reminder to, then tap 'new reminder' at the bottom of the screen.

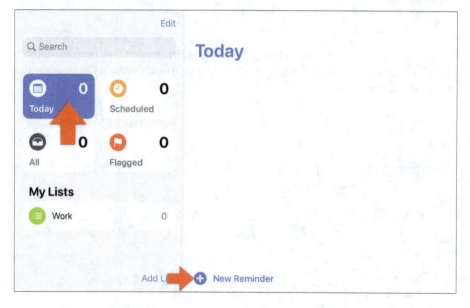

Type in your reminder. Tap 'done' on the top right when you're finished.

Create a New List

Tap 'add list' at the bottom of the screen if you want to create a new one.

Enter a name for your list at the top, then select a colour and an icon to represent your list.

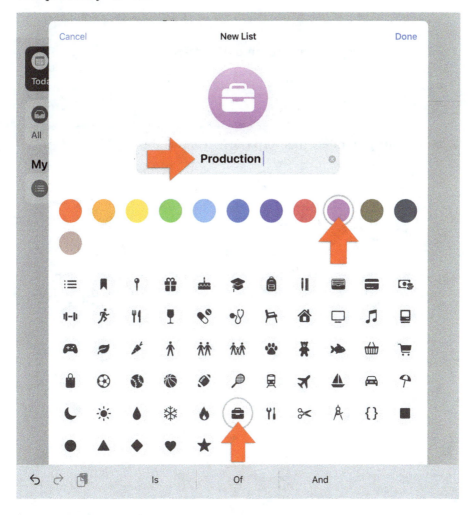

Tap 'done' on the top right when you're finished.

Your lists will appear under the 'my lists' section on the side panel of the reminders app.

Schedule a Reminder

You can schedule a reminder to remind you of something on a particular day. To do this, tap the list you want to add the reminder to.

Tap 'new reminder' at the bottom of the screen.

Type in your reminder, then tap the 'i' icon on the right.

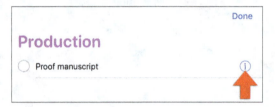

Tap 'remind me on a day', then on the next window tap 'remind me at a time'. Tap 'alarm', then select the date and time using the sliders.

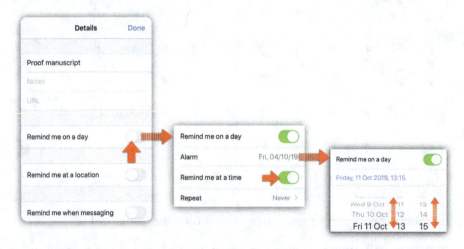

Tap 'done' when you're finished.

Reminder When Messaging Someone

You can schedule a reminder to remind you of something when contacting a particular person on your contacts list. To do this, tap the list you want to add the reminder to.

Tap 'new reminder' at the bottom of the screen.

Type in your reminder, then tap the 'i' icon on the right.

From the drop down, tap 'remind me when messaging' (you may need to scroll down a bit)

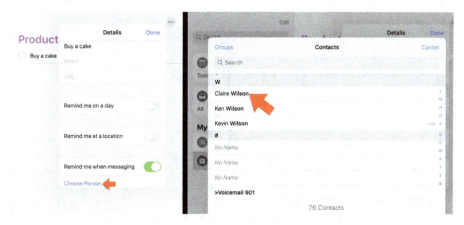

Select the person's name from your contacts list. Now the next time you contact this person, you'll get a reminder.

Reminder at a Location

You can schedule a reminder to remind you of something when you are at a particular location. To do this, tap the list you want to add the reminder to.

Tap 'new reminder' at the bottom of the screen.

Type in your reminder, then tap the 'i' icon on the right. From the drop down, tap 'remind me at a location', then tap 'location'.

Type in the address, select the closest match from the suggestions.

Tap 'arriving' to remind you when you arrive at the destination. Tap 'leaving' if you want to be reminded when you leave the destination. You can also set the distance from the location that triggers the reminder - in the example above, you'll be reminded when you're 524.9ft away. Tap the black circle on the location map and drag it bigger or smaller.

Tap 'details' to go back, then tap 'done'.

Maps

Maps is an extremely useful app if you are trying to find out where a particular place is and need to find driving directions. It works like a SatNav/GPS giving you precise directions straight from door to door.

Using the panel on the left hand side, you can search for a location - just type in an address, or place name. Under that, you can add a 'home' location, and a 'work' location. This allows you to tap 'home' or 'work' to find that location and is useful if you want directions to that place, or traffic reports between 'home' and 'work'. You can also add favourite locations, ie locations you travel to regularly.

You can view the map in three different types - tap the 'i' icon on the top right of the screen to change this.

Select a map type from the options.

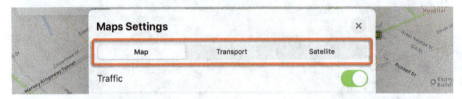

Here below, you can see the different maps: street map, transport map, and satellite map.

Street maps are great if you are using the maps app as a GPS/Satnav while driving.

Transport maps give you public transport routes in a particular location for buses and trains. You'd be wise to check local public transport information for updates and changes.

Satellite maps are great if you are exploring a city or area of interest as well as planning a route. You can see these maps in 2D and 3D.

Driving Directions

To find driving directions, type in your destination into the search field on the top left of the screen and select the destination from the list of suggestions.

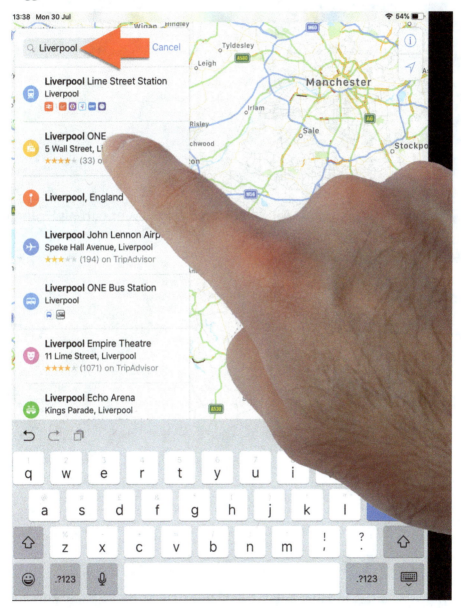

Select 'directions' from the destination sidebar.

By default, the maps app will start the route from your current location - you can change this, just type in another location.

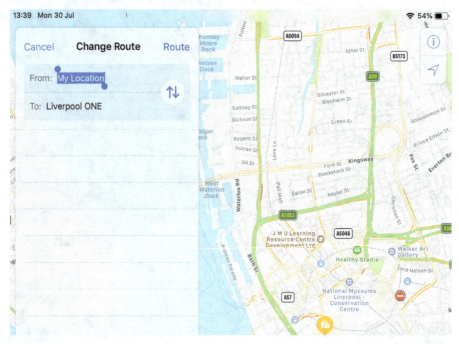

Tap on 'route' to calculate a route between your location and the destination you entered earlier.

Along the bottom of the screen, you'll see 'drive', 'walk', and 'transport'.

This allows you to get directions for driving, if you're walking, or if you're taking public transport. For this demo, we're looking for driving directions, so we'll keep the option set to 'drive'.

On the screen you'll see an overview of your route. You can zoom in and out or move around the map using your finger to see details or roads.

From options on the left hand side of the screen, select the best route if there is more than one route.

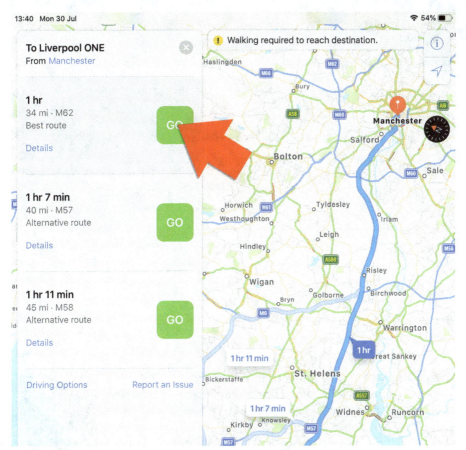

Chapter 6: Common Apps

Here you'll see the start of your route, with turn by turn directions that will automatically change as you drive along the route.

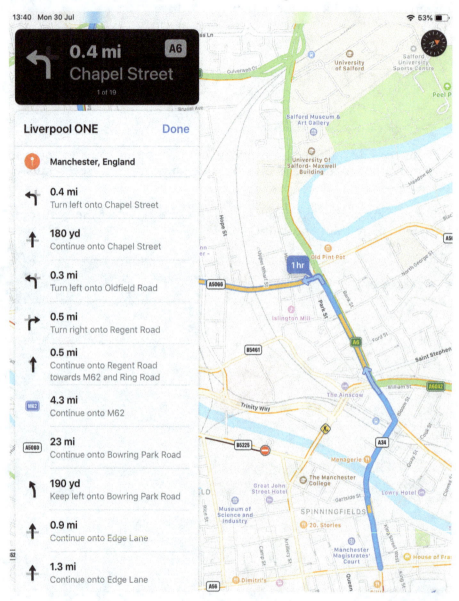

Take a look at the 'Exploring Maps' demo in the 'using iPad' section of the accompanying video resources. Scan the code or go to the following website

www.elluminetpress.com/using-iPad-pro

3D Maps

3D maps are a great way to explore landmarks, major cities and areas of interest. You can flyover a city and explore what it has to offer.

To do this, first change your map to a satellite map if you haven't already done so. Then tap the 3D icon on the right hand side to switch to 3D mode.

Type in a city name, place name or address into the search field on the top left of the screen.

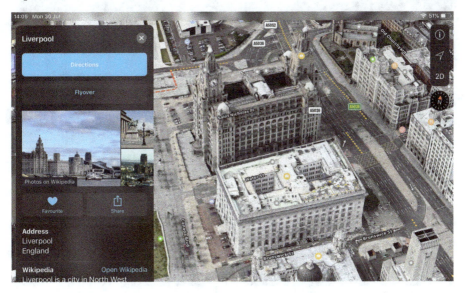

You can zoom in and out of the 3D map and move around using your finger

To take a flyover tour, tap 'flyover' in the info side panel.

Now move your iPad around, as you do this you'll notice the view move on your iPad. Use your finger to zoom in and out or move up and down the view.

Tap once anywhere on the screen to reveal the popup menu on the bottom left.

Tap 'start city tour' if available for that city to watch an animated 3D tour of the city.

Tap the x to close the flyover view.

News App

The news app collects breaking stories from around the world and locally into one app, based on the topics you are interested in.

When you first start the app, you'll see a list of top stories, trending stories, and stories recommended for you. Scroll down the page, tap on a story to read the details.

To open the side panel, tap the icon on the top left of the screen

From here you can select different news sources, magazines, newspapers and websites.

You can also search for specific channels. To reveal the search field if it isn't already visible, swipe downwards on the side panel, the search field will appear at the top. Type in your search.

To personalise your news, tap the channels icon on the top left of the screen.

From the slideout list, scroll down to 'suggested by siri' and tap the heart icon next to the channels you're interested in.

Scroll down to the bottom, then tap 'discover channels & topics'.

From here you can select different news sources, magazines, newspapers and websites.

Tap 'done' at the bottom of the screen when you're finished.

Apple Books App

Formerly known as iBooks, Apple Books is your electronic bookshelf and allows you to read ebooks. Tap the icon on your home screen.

You can download hundreds of different e-books that are available in the bookstore; from the latest novels, food, kids books or manuals.

Along the bottom of the screen you'll see some icons. Here you can see the books you are 'reading now', browse your library of books you've downloaded, browse the book store, look at audio books and search for a specific book title or author.

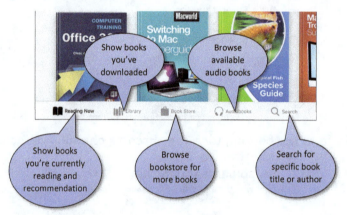

Just tap on the book cover to open the book.

Browse the Store

You can also browse through the book store. To do this, tap 'bookstore' icon on the panel along the bottom of the screen.

Click 'browse sections' to reveal the categories in the bookstore. Now select a category. Perhaps you're into 'crime thrillers', 'fiction', or 'education'. Just tap on a category to view the available books.

Search the Store

You can also search for specific authors or titles. To do this tap on the 'search' icon on the panel along the bottom of the screen.

Then type what you're looking for in the search field at the top of the screen.

Tap on a book cover to see more details.

From this page you'll be able to read a sample, the book's description, read any reviews, and buy/download the book.

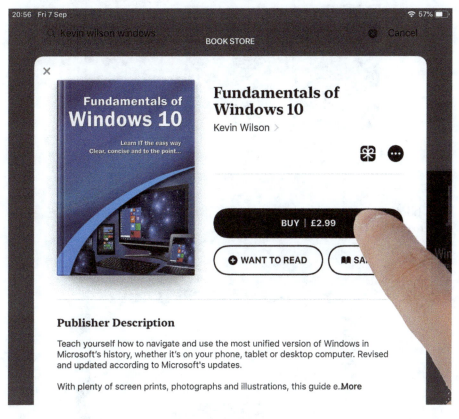

Tap 'get' if the book is free, or tap the price tag to download the book to your library. Once you've downloaded the book, you'll find it in your library. Tap the library icon on the panel along the bottom of the screen.

Tap on the book cover to begin reading.

The book will open up full screen. Swipe left or right across the screen to turn the pages.

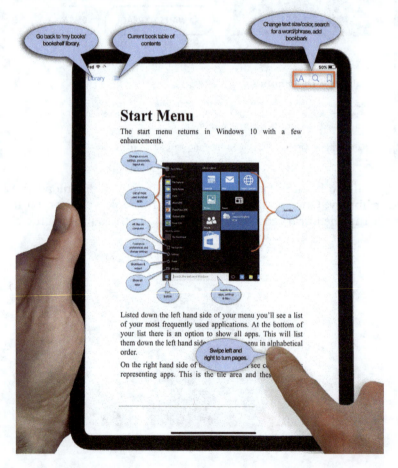

Files App

The iCloud Drive App has been dropped and replaced with the Files App. You'll find the icon on your dock.

In the Files App, you'll find all your files that are stored on your iPad and iCloud Drive. The Files App works best if you hold your iPad horizontally.

When you first open the files app, you'll see your most recently opened documents. To see all your files tap 'browse' on the panel along the bottom of the screen.

To see all the documents stored on iCloud, tap 'iCloud Drive' from the panel along the left hand side of the screen.

To see files saved physically on your iPad, tap 'on my iPad'.

To find any files downloaded with Safari web browser, tap 'downloads'.

Tap on any icon to open the folder or file.

Create New Folders

You can also create your own folders. To create a new folder, tap on the location you want the new folder to appear in, eg 'pictures' folder on iCloud drive.

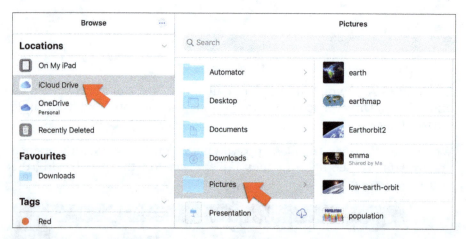

Tap and hold your finger on the blank space at the bottom of the file list. Tap 'new folder' from the popup.

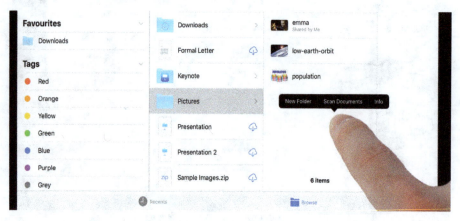

Enter a name for your folder. Tap 'done' on the top right.

Drag Files into Folders

You can drag and drop files into these folders. Tap and hold your finger on the file, then drag your finger across the glass to the folder you want to put the file into. In this example, I'm going to drag and drop a photo into the 'Summer' folder.

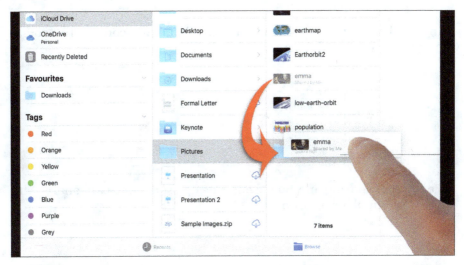

Tap on the folders to open them, tap on the file thumbnails to open the files.

Delete Files or Folders

You can also delete files. Tap 'select' on the top right of the screen.

Tap on the files you want to delete.

Tap the delete icon on the toolbar along the bottom of the screen.

Share a File

Tap 'select' on the top right of the screen.

Tap the file you want to share, then tap the share icon on the toolbar along the bottom of the screen.

Select your sharing method from the options. You can share with iMessage, email, or airdrop.

You can also share folders with friends, family and colleagues using iCloud Drive.

External Drive Support

You can access files on a USB drive, SD card or hard drive. Plug your device into the USB-C port on the bottom of your iPad. If your USB device isn't USB-C, then you'll need a USB-C to USB adapter.

Plug the adapter into the docking port on the bottom of your iPad. With this, you can plug in a standard USB external drive, SD card reader, or USB drive.

Your drive will appear under 'locations' on the side panel of your files app. Tap on the device to view files and folders stored on the drive.

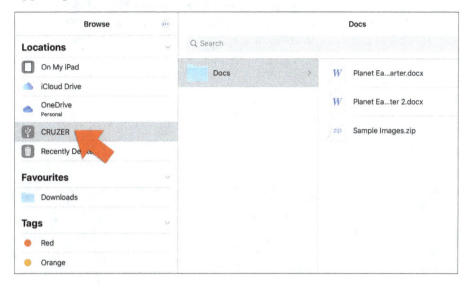

You can drag and drop files onto the USB device.

Rename Files or Folders

Tap and hold your finger on a file or folder, then select 'rename' from the pop up menu.

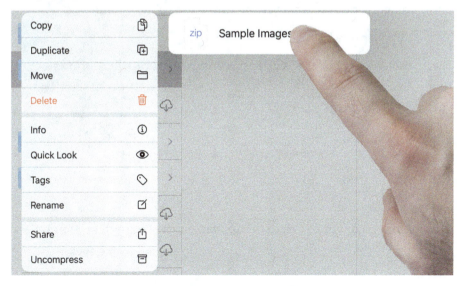

Type in the new name for the folder or file.

File Servers

You can connect to a file server at work or a home PC using the SMB protocol. To connect to a server, tap the 3 dots icon on the top right of the left hand pane. From the drop down, tap 'connect to server'.

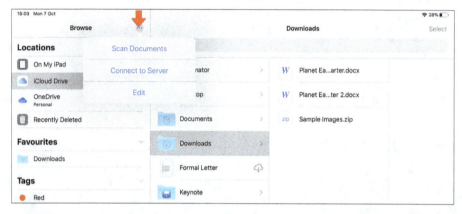

Enter the server's address.

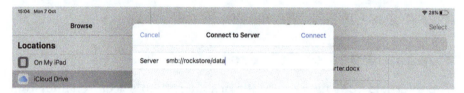

For example, if I wanted to connect to my file server on the network, I'd enter the server name followed by the shared folder name.

```
smb://rockstore/data
```

Enter the shared folder's username and password when prompted.

Once connected, your folder will appear on the 'shared' section on the left hand pane.

Apple Pay

Apple Pay allows you to keep digital copies of your bank cards, and lets you pay for things using your iPhone or iPad. You can use this feature on an iPad but it is more convenient with an iPhone.

Apple Pay will run on iPhone SE, iPhone 6, iPhone 6 Plus, and later as well as, iPad Pro, iPad Air 2, iPad mini 3, and later.

Setup

Make sure your bank supports Apple Pay. If so, go to your settings app then scroll down the left hand side and tap 'wallet & apple pay'. Then tap 'add credit or debit card' link. Tap 'continue' on the apple pay popup.

Now, in the 'add card' window, if you already have a credit/debit card registered with your Apple ID, then apple pay will ask you to add this one.

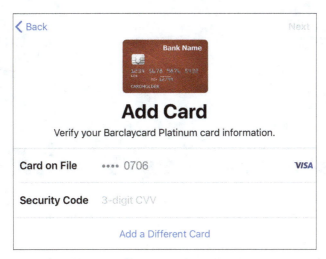

If this is the card you want to use, then enter the 3 digit security code and tap 'next' on the top right. Hit 'agree' on the terms and conditions; your card will be added.

If you want to add a different card, tap 'add a different card', at the bottom of the 'add card' window. You can scan your card with the iPad's camera.

Position the card so it fills the white rectangle on your screen. Apple Pay will scan your card and automatically enter your details

If you can't get the camera to scan the card, tap 'enter card details manually' then key in your card number, exp dates and so on.

Enter the security code from the back of your card. The bank will authorise your card. Accept the terms and conditions.

If you also have an iPhone, these cards will be synced with your iPhone so you can use Apple Pay on there too.

Using Apple Pay

You can use Apple Pay at any store that supports this feature. You will usually see the logo displayed in store. You can also use Apple Pay on some online stores.

To pay with Apple Pay, place your iPhone/iPad above the reader with your thumb on the home button without pressing it. You'll see a prompt on your iPhone for the amount - you authorise the payment using the finger print scanner on the home button.

If you want to pay with a card other than the default, hold the top of your iPhone near the contactless reader without touching the home button.

Tap the card you want to use.

Present your iPhone to the contactless reader with your thumb on the home button to complete payment.

Holding your thumb on the home button uses the finger print reader to verify your identity and is sometimes called 'touch id'.

Voice Memos

You can record audio using your iPad's built in mic or a bluetooth external mic. You can record voice memos, meetings and lectures.

You'll find the voice memo app on your home screen.

Lets take a look at the main screen. Here you can see your previous recordings listed down the left hand side. Any recording you select here will appear in the white panel on the right hand side of the screen.

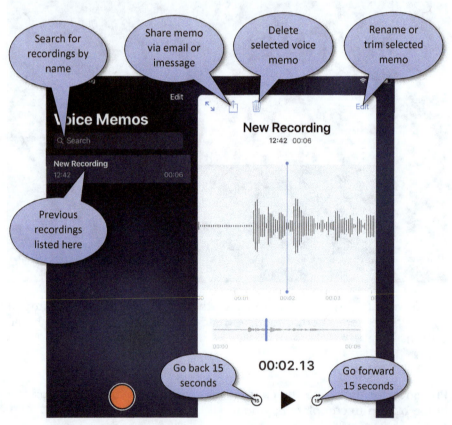

Tap the play button in the grey panel on the right to playback the recording.

Recording Memos

To record a memo, simply tap the red record button on the bottom left of the screen.

The memo app will start recording. You'll see a wave form appear in the middle of the screen to indicate the app is picking up audio.

To pause a recording temporarily, tap the pause icon on the left. To stop the recording, tap 'done'.

Your memo will appear in the list on the left hand side of the main screen.

Renaming Memos

The first thing you should do with a new voice memo recording is give it a meaningful name. The last thing you want is every memo called 'new recording.

To demonstrate this, we'll rename the voice memo we just recorded. Select the voice memo from the list on the left hand side. Then tap and hold your finger on the name in the right hand panel, until the keyboard pops up.

Delete the default text, then type in a meaningful name for the recording. Tap enter on the on-screen keyboard to confirm the name.

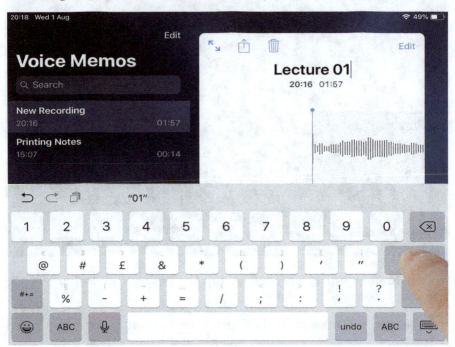

Trim a Memo

You can trim the beginning and the ends of the memo voice recording. To do this, select the recording you want to trim from the list on the left hand side of the main screen. Then tap edit on the top right of the grey panel on the right hand side.

Tap the trim icon on the top right

Now to trim the beginning and ends of the clip, drag the yellow handles along the track until you get to the start and end points you want.

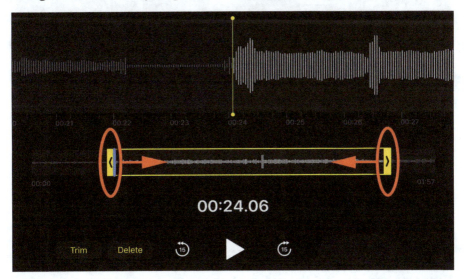

Tap 'trim' when you're done.

Measure App

The Measure App uses augmented reality to measure distances and objects. I still prefer a good ol' tape measure but let's take a look at the app anyway.

You'll find the Measure App on your home screen.

Point your iPad's camera at the object you want to measure. The Measure App will auto detect any geometric shapes such as the ones on the shelves in the example below. Tap the screen to confirm the detected shape. This will create a mask.

At the edges of the mask, you'll see some small white dots. Tap and drag these to make sure it fully covers the section you want to measure.

Now you can see on the sides of the mask, the Measure App has measured the distances. This particular area is 44cm by 41cm.

You can add points to measure distances between them. To do this, tap the white + icon on the right hand side. You'll see a white dot appear on the screen. Tap the white + icon again to add another point.

Now tap and drag the white points to the edges of the object you want to measure - you'll notice a line will form between them. In the example here, I'm measuring the height of the shelf - so I'm going to drag one point to the top of the shelf, and the other point to the bottom.

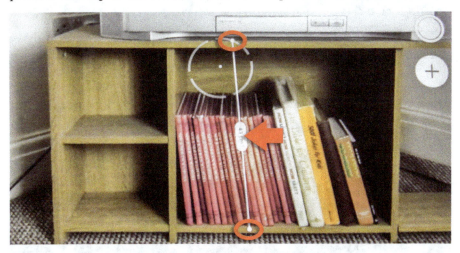

You can see the height of this particular shelf is 43cm. Not 100% accurate yet, the shelf measured to the same points as above with a measuring tape was 49cm, so I wouldn't rely on it if you're doing a bit of DIY.

Clock App

You can use the clock app to set alarms, timers, as a stop watch, and create time zone clocks so you can see the time in other countries.

You'll find the clock app on your home screen.

World Clock

With world clock, you can create clocks for any city or country in the world. This is useful if you have friends or family in another country, so you know what time it is there and don't call them in the middle of the night. It's also useful if you're travelling.

To see the world clock, tap 'world clock' on the panel along the bottom of the screen.

To add a clock, tap the + sign on the top right of the screen.

Type in the name of the city or country you want to add

Tap the name of the city/country in the list of suggestions.

Now you'll see the clock appear on the map.

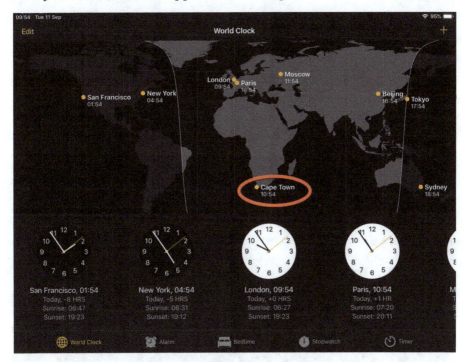

To remove a clock, just tap 'edit' on the top left and you'll see a small red sign appear on the top left of each clock. Tap the red sign to remove it.

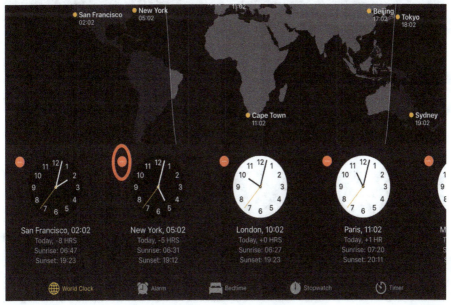

Alarm

You can also set multiple alarms. Eg one for wake up. To do this, select 'alarm' from the panel along the bottom of the screen.

This will display all the alarms you have set.

To set a new alarm, tap the + sign on the top right.

Set the alarm to the time you want the alarm to go off. Tap 'repeat' to set what days you want the alarm, eg 'weekdays'. Tap 'label' to name the alarm, eg 'wakeup'. Tap 'sound' to choose what your alarm sounds like - you can select a sound or a song from your music library. Tap 'save' on the top right when you're done.

You'll see the alarms you've added. Tap the green slider on the alarm to turn it on and off.

Bed Time

Bed time allows you to create a sleep routine, allowing you to set a time to go to bed and a time to wake up, and the clock app will remind you.

Select 'bed time' from the panel along the bottom of the screen.

The first time you run this feature, you'll need to go through the setup. To do this tap 'get started'. Select the time you want to wake up using the sliders on the screen. Tap 'next'

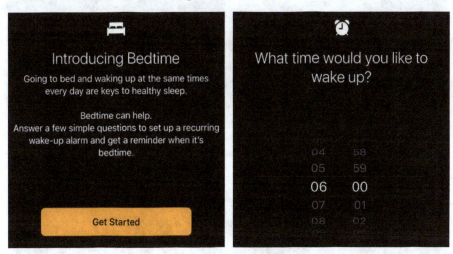

Select the days of the week, then select the number of hours sleep you need. Usually 8 hours. Tap 'next'.

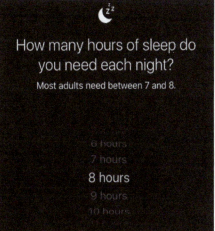

Set the days of the week you want your routine to be in force. Tap 'next'.

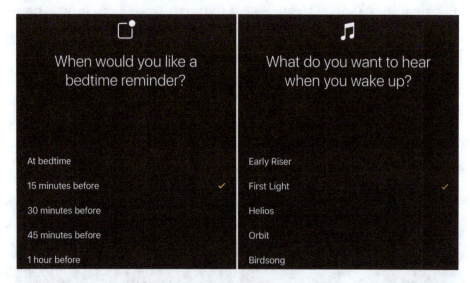

Once you've completed the setup, you can see your bedtime on the main screen. To adjust the bedtime time, drag the sleep marker around the clock. Similarly to adjust your wakeup time, drag the wake marker around the clock.

To change your options, tap 'options' on the top left of the screen. Here you can change the days of the week, set a reminder and set a wake up sound.

Stop Watch

Use the stopwatch to time events. Eg an athletics event. Select 'stopwatch' from the panel along the bottom of the screen.

Tap 'start/stop' to start and stop the timer.

Tap 'lap' to count the number of laps if you are timing a sporting event such as athletics or racing.

Timer

Use the timer to set a count down timer. Select 'timer' from the panel along the bottom of the screen. Use the sliders to select the length of time in hours, minutes and seconds. For example, if you're playing a game or timing an egg, just set the amount of time allowed.

Tap 'start' to start the count down. Tap the iTunes icon next to where it says 'constellation' to change the sound the timer makes when the time runs out.

Productivity Apps

Apple have developed three productivity apps that allow you to create documents and keynote presentations.

These apps don't usually come pre-installed, so you will need to download them from the app store. Open the app store and search for iWork, then download Pages, Keynote and Numbers.

In this chapter, we'll take a look at getting started with these three apps.

Let's start with Pages.

Pages Word Processing

To launch Pages, tap the icon on your home screen.

Once Pages has opened, tap 'continue' on the welcome page. You'll see your most recently opened documents, you'll also be able to browse through your documents, and create new blank documents or one from a template. Tap 'browse' on the bottom right of the screen.

Tap 'create new document'.

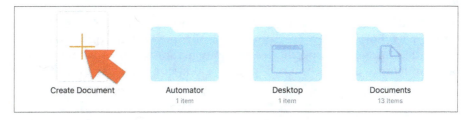

Select a template, or tap 'blank' to start a new document.

Chapter 7: Productivity Apps

Once you have selected the template to use you will see the main work screen. Let's take a closer look at the main editing screen.

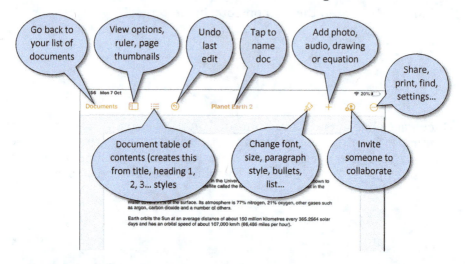

You'll find your toolbar across the top of the screen where you'll find your tools for formatting your text.

Along the bottom, you'll see your on-screen keyboard. Along the top of your keyboard there are some icons. From the left you have, tabs, indents, change font, predictive text suggestions, font size, text align, and an icon to add comments, page breaks, contents page etc.

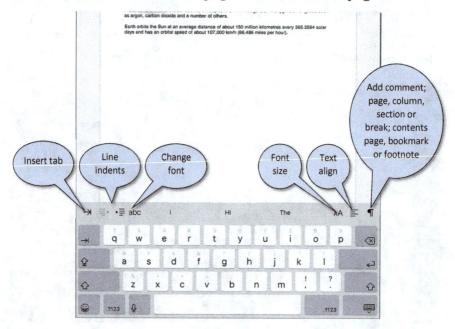

Formatting Text

Begin typing in your text into the main window as shown above.

The text we entered needs formatting. To add a heading, type it in above the block of text.

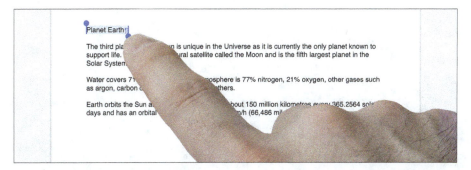

Highlight your text with your finger as shown above by dragging the blue dots over the text, then tap the paint brush from the toolbar.

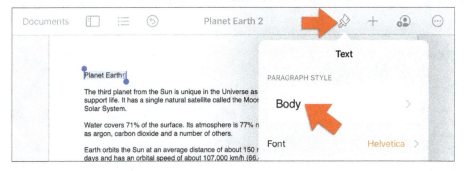

Tap 'title' to change the title style of the selected text.

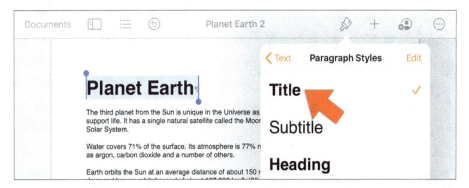

Make sure you use the correct heading styles for different parts of your document, so Pages can automatically generate a table of contents.

Using this menu, you can also change the font, font size, font colour, text alignment (left, center, right), line spacing, bullet lists, and columns.

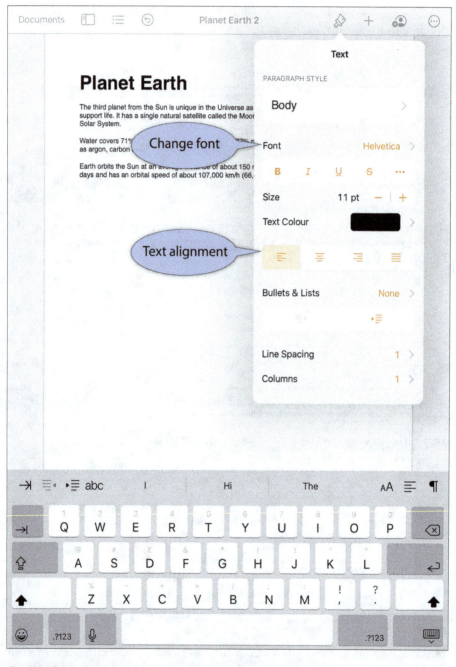

Just select the icon from the drop down menu.

Adding a Picture

The easiest way to add a picture is to tap the plus sign on the right hand side of the toolbar. Then from the dropdown, tap the image icon on the right. Select one of your albums if you want to insert a photo you took with your camera or tap 'insert from' if you have an image on your iCloud drive. Tap your pictures folder and select an image.

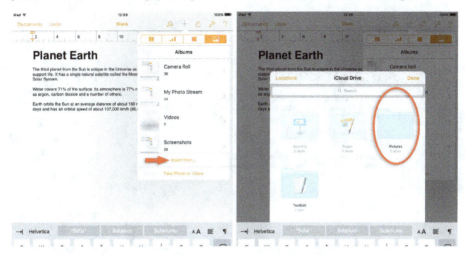

You can resize your image by clicking the resize handles, circled below, and dragging them.

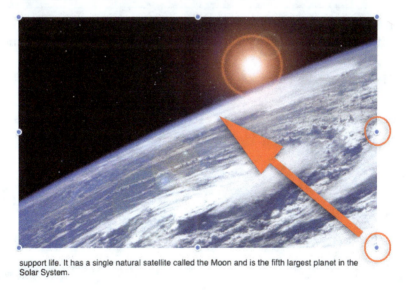

support life. It has a single natural satellite called the Moon and is the fifth largest planet in the Solar System.

You can change the styles by adding borders and shadows by tapping on the paint brush icon on the top right of your toolbar.

Collaboration

You can invite people to collaborate with you on your document. This works well for group projects where more than one person can edit a document at the same time. To invite people, open your document then tap the 'people' icon on the top right.

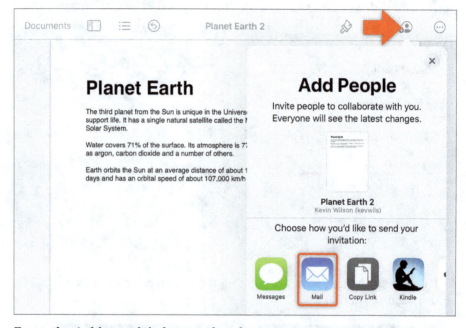

From the 'add people' sheet, select how you want to send the invite - use either email or messages. Add the person's email address and tap send.

When the other person accepts the invitation, they can edit your document

Keynote Presentations

Keynote allows you to create multimedia presentations. To launch keynote, go to your home screen and tap keynote.

Tap continue if you're running keynote for the first time. You'll see your most recently opened presentations, you'll also be able to browse through your presentations, and create new blank ones or one from a template. Tap 'browse' on the bottom right of the screen.

Tap 'create presentation'.

From here you can select from a variety of pre-designed templates with different themes, fonts and colours.

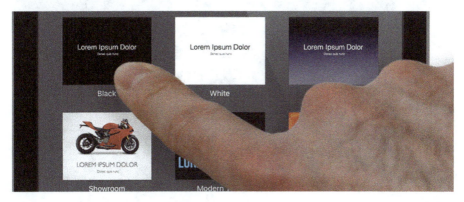

Once you have selected a template you will see the main screen as shown below. This is where you can start building your presentation.

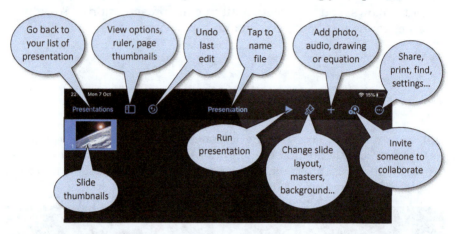

Editing a Slide

Double tap in the heading field shown below and enter a heading eg 'Planet Earth'. You can tap and drag the heading wherever you like.

Adding a New Slide

Tap the new slide button located on the bottom left of the screen, then tap a slide layout from the options that appear.

Add some text by double clicking on the text box that appears in the slide.

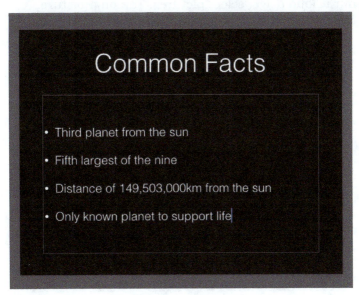

Adding Media

To add images and media to your slide, tap the plus sign on your tool bar at the top right of your screen. Then tap the image icon on the right.

If you want to add one of your photographs from your photo library, tap on one of your albums and select 'photo or video'. If you want to insert a picture from your iCloud, tap 'insert from...'. If you want to take a new picture, tap camera, if you want to add audio, tap 'record audio'...

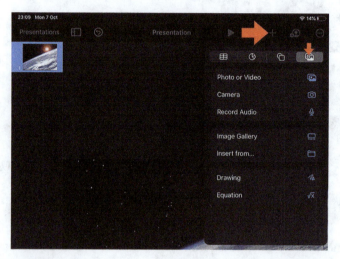

From your iCloud drive, select pictures. Tap on a picture.

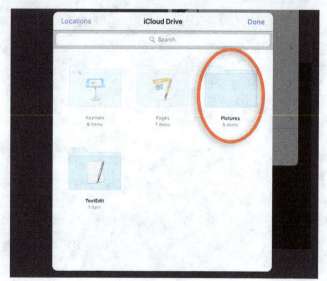

Animations

Animations allow you to make objects such as text or photographs appear...

Tap on your text box and select the animate icon located on the top right corner of your screen

Then tap 'add build in'

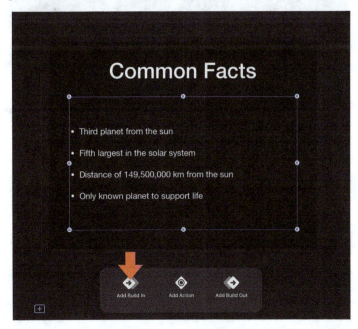

Then select an effect you want, eg 'appear'.

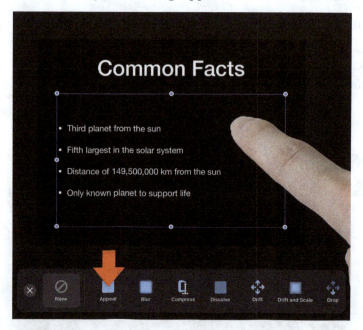

Tap on your slide, then tap 'appear' again to specify that you want the bullet points to appear one by one. Tap 'delivery' and select 'by bullet'.

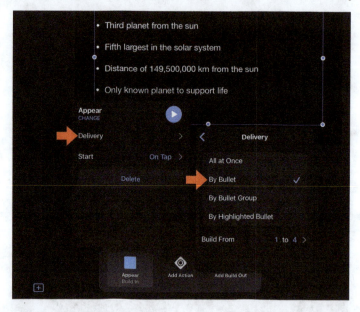

To see what the effect looks like, tap the play button on the top right of your screen.

Formatting Text Boxes

Tap on a text box you want to format. You can add borders to your text boxes, reflection effects or background colours.

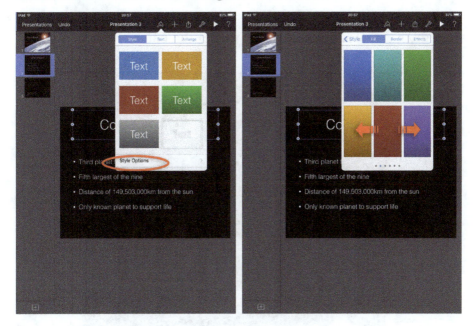

To format the border and fill your text box, tap your text box and tap the paint brush icon, on the top right of the screen.

Tap fill to change the background colour of the text box. Then swipe your finger across the selections of effects and tap on one to select it. In this example, I am going for a nice blue gradient fill.

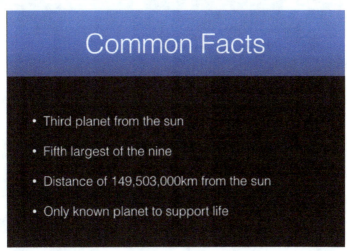

Formatting Text Inside Textboxes

To change the formatting of the text, for example to change the colour of the text or make it bold.

First select your text in the text box you want to change. Tap on the text three times to select it all. Then tap the paint brush icon on the top right of your toolbar.

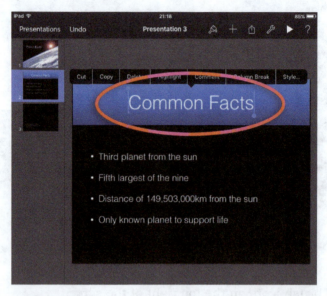

From here you can change the font, the font colour, size etc.

As an example I have changed the colour to light blue and made it bold.

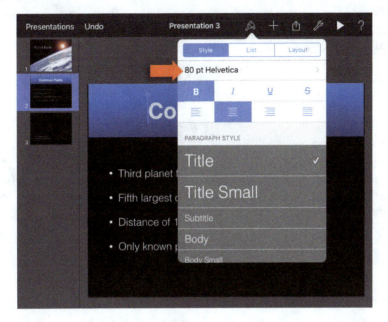

Tap on the font name, illustrated with the red arrow in the image above. Then from here you can change the size, the colour and the typeface.

Tap the colour and select a colour. Do the same for 'font' - tap font and select a font.

Numbers Spreadsheets

Numbers is a spreadsheet program that allows you analyse and present information. To launch Numbers, go to your home screen and tap 'numbers'.

Tap continue if you're running keynote for the first time. You'll see your most recently opened presentations, you'll also be able to browse through your spreadsheets, and create new blank ones or one from a template. Tap 'browse' on the bottom right of the screen.

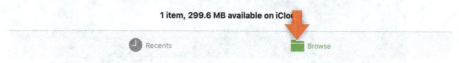

Tap 'create spreadsheet'.

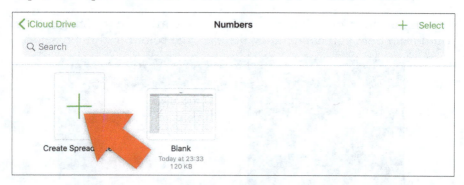

From here you can select from a variety of pre-designed templates with different themes, fonts and colours.

Once you have selected a template you will see the main screen as shown below. This is where you can start building your spreadsheet.

Let's take a closer look at the different tools available on the numbers main screen.

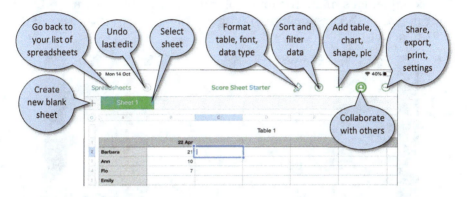

Entering Data

In the example, we are going to create a basic scoring sheet. When you tap inside a cell on your spreadsheet, you'll see the on-screen keyboard show up. This will allow you to enter data.

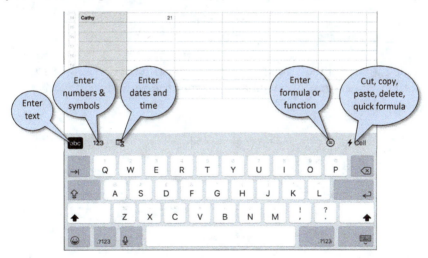

Along the top of the on-screen keyboard, you'll see an icon for entering text, numbers or symbols, dates and times. On the other side, you will find tools to enter formulas as well as copy and paste tools.

Just tap in a cell, select the type of data you want to enter from the bar along the top of the keyboard, then type it in using the on-screen keyboard.

Simple Text Formatting

Sometimes it improves the readability of your spreadsheet to format the data in the cells.

For example, let's make the total column bold. To do this tap and hold your finger on the first cell, then drag your finger across the rest of the cells to select them.

Tap the format icon on the top right

Select the 'cell' tab. Tap the bold icon. You can also change the text colour, size and font, as well as alignment, and wrap

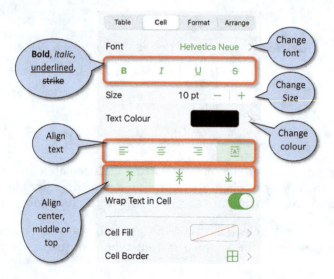

Resizing Rows and Columns

You can resize a column or row by clicking and dragging the column or row handle. To resize, tap on a column, you'll see a small handle appear.

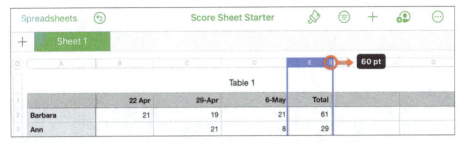

Do the same for resizing rows.

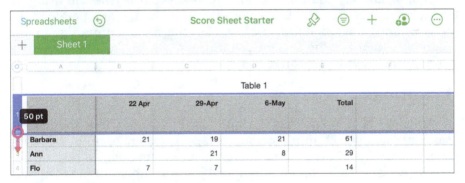

Inserting Rows & Columns

To insert a row between Flo and Emily, tap the row 'flo' is in, then tap the green 'row' icon on the bottom right of your screen.

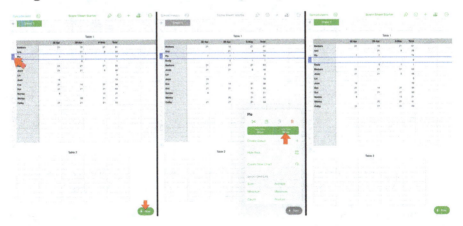

Tap 'add row below'. Use the same procedure for columns.

Formulas

You can add formulas to manipulate data. For example, if I had two numbers and wanted to find the difference, I could subtract one number from the other.

First, tap in the cell you want the solution to appear in, then tap the '=' sign on the top right of the on-screen keyboard. This will bring up the formula bar. Tap the first cell in the formula, tap an operator from the bar along the top of the on-screen keyboard (the minus sign in this example), then tap the second cell in the formula. Tap the green tick icon on the right when you're finished.

Functions

A function is a predefined formula that you can use to perform calculations and manipulate your data. For example, on our scoring sheet I can create another column and use a function to add up the scores. To insert a function, tap the cell you want the solution to appear in, then tap the '=' sign on the top right of the on-screen keyboard, then tap the 'fx' icon on the left hand side.

Tap 'sum'. Now, tap and drag your finger over the values you want to apply the function to. Tap the green tick on the right to finish.

You can also find other functions, just tap 'categories' and browse through the functions.

Fonts

Apple has added a feature allowing users to install third party fonts in iPadOS. First, you'll need to download a font management app from the app store. To do this, open your app store, select 'search' and search for 'ifont'. There are others available but most are rubbish. I found ifont easiest to use and the app is free.

Tap 'get' to download the app.

The app will appear on your home screen once installed. Tap on the icon to start the app. Let's take a look at the app

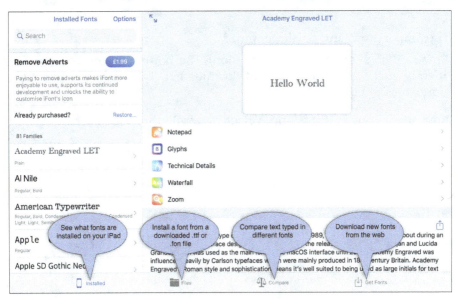

Using the menu bar along the bottom you can install fonts and download fonts.

Downloading

To download new fonts, tap 'get fonts', then tap a site to download the fonts from. Eg 'Dafont'

Tap in the search field on the top right of the screen and enter the font name you want to download.

Tap 'import to iFont' on the popup.

Now tap 'files' on the menu bar along the bottom of the screen. Tap 'install' next to the font you just downloaded. Tap 'allow', 'close', then 'done' on the popups.

Now, open your settings app, select 'general', then tap 'profile'.

Tap 'install' on the top right of the screen.

Installing from File

If you've downloaded a font file from Safari, open the ifont app select 'get fonts' from the menu bar along the bottom of the screen.

Select 'open files' on the top left. Navigate to your downloads folder and select the font file you want to install.

Select 'files' from the menu bar along the bottom of the screen.

Tap 'download' next to the font you just installed.

Tap 'allow', 'close', then 'done' on the popups.

Now, open your settings app, select 'general', then tap 'profile'.

Tap 'install' on the top right of the screen.

Printing Documents

To print documents from an iPad you'll need a printer that is compatible with Air Print. Most modern printers will have this feature included.

Air Print

If your printer is Air Print enabled, then your printer will show up in the print dialog box automatically.

To print a document, select the share icon, then tap 'print'. If you're using the Pages App, select the '...' icon and tap 'print'.

Select your printer from the printer field, enter the number of copies you want, and select the page range you want to print (eg pages 2-4), or leave it on 'all pages', if you want the whole document.

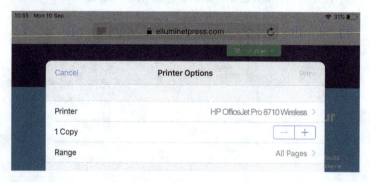

Tap 'print' on the top right when you're done.

Older Printers

If your printer doesn't have the Air Print feature, you can download an app from the App Store for your printer.

- **HP Printers** download **HP Smart**

- **Samsung Printers** download **Samsung Mobile Print**

- **Epson Printers** download **Epson iPrint**

- **Canon Printers** download **Canon Print**

Open the app on your iPad and select the document you want to print.

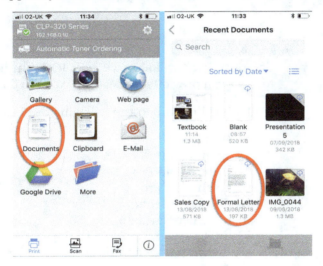

Select print.

Chapter 8

Maintaining Your iPad

The new iPads will ship with iPadOS, but if you need to update a previous model then you can do that here.

iPadOS will install on the following devices.

12.9-inch iPad Pro
11-inch iPad Pro
10.5-inch iPad Pro
9.7-inch iPad Pro
iPad (7th generation)
iPad (6th generation)
iPad (5th generation)
iPad mini (5th generation)
iPad mini 4
iPad Air (3rd generation)
iPad Air 2

Before upgrading, make sure you have some time where you don't need to use your iPad as it will be temporarily inoperative while the installation takes place.

iPad Backups

You can backup your settings, apps and files to your iCloud account. Go to Settings, Tap on your account name, select 'iCloud', then sign in if you haven't already done so.

Select 'iCloud Backup'.

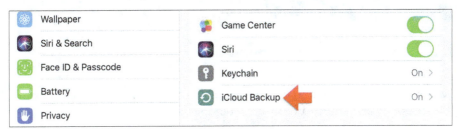

Turn on iCloud Backup if it isn't already. Tap 'Back Up Now'.

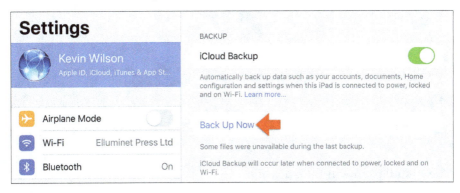

System Updates

To run the update, on your iPad open your settings app. Tap 'general' then select 'Software Update'.

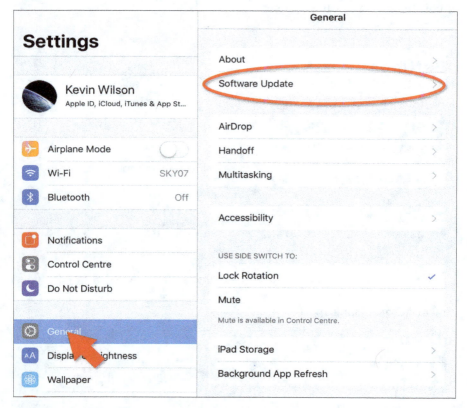

Make sure your device is connected to both Wi-Fi and a power supply, then tap 'download and install' to begin.

The installation will take a while.

If you prefer to update using iTunes. Connect your iPad to a USB port on your computer using the cable. Tap the iPad icon on the top left of the toolbar.

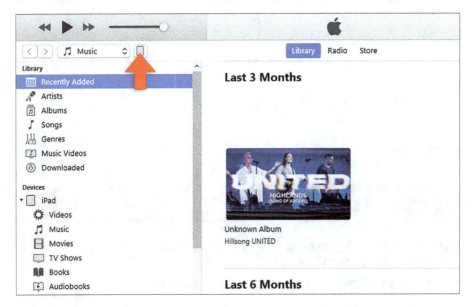

In the summary section, click 'Check for Update', then choose 'Download and Install'.

Click 'update' if prompted.

Confirm your iCloud details. Your iPad will restart automatically.

You may have to run through the initial setup again on page 21. After this, your iPad is ready to use.

App Updates

To check for app updates, open the app store

Tap your Apple ID icon on the top right of the screen.

Scroll down to 'upcoming automatic updates'. You'll see a list of updates that are pending.

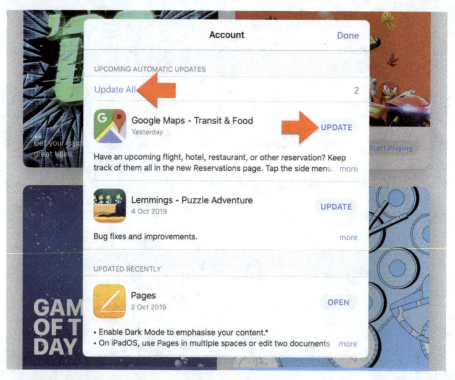

Tap 'update' next to the app to update, or tap 'update all' to apply all the updates that are available.

Deleting Apps

To delete apps, tap and hold your finger on an app, until the X appears on the top left of the icon.

Tap on the X to delete the app. Tap 'done' on the top right when you're finished.

You can also delete any of the pre-installed apps you don't use, in the same way as above.

iPad Storage Maintenance

You can see what apps an data are stored on your iPad's physical storage. First open your settings app, select 'general', then 'ipad storage'

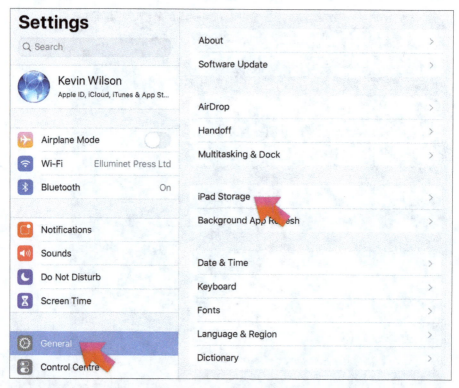

From here, you can see all the apps installed on your iPad. You can also delete or offload apps that you don't use.

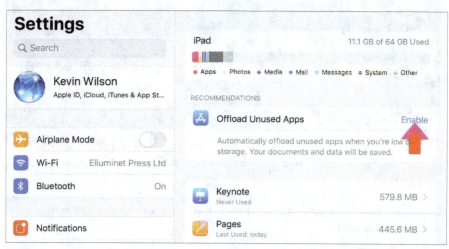

Tap 'enable' next to 'offload unused apps'. This will automatically offload apps you don't use but only when you run out of storage. When apps are offloaded, the app itself is deleted from your iPad freeing up space, but any associated documents and data remain. The app icon remains on the home screen, so you can still access it.

When you tap on an offloaded app it will automatically re-install and any documents and data will still be there.

Listed below that on the 'ipad storage' screen are all the apps installed on your iPad. Tap on an app name to see details.

At the top you'll see the amount of space the app takes up (the app size), and the space used for documents and data. From here you can manually offload the app, or delete it. To do this, tap 'offload app' to offload, and 'delete app' to delete.

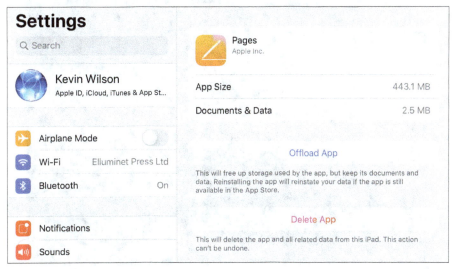

iPad Recovery

First plug your USB cable into your mac. Power up and, unlock your iPad.

Press and release the volume up button, then press and release the volume down button. Press and hold the power button until you see the recovery screen.

Ignore the shutdown slider that pops up on the screen, keep holding the power button until you see the restore screen.

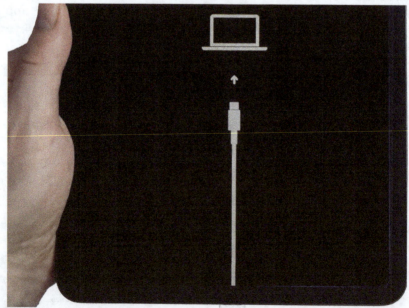

On your mac, you'll see a prompt appear in the finder app.

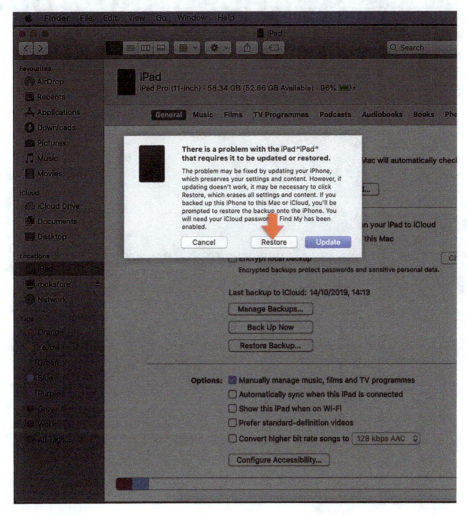

Tap 'restore' to restore your iPad to factory defaults.

Chapter 9

Accessorise Your iPad

There are thousands of different accessories available for the iPad and you can buy them from a number of different manufacturers, not only Apple.

You just need to keep in mind the size and model of your iPad when shopping for accessories. Make sure it will fit the model you have - iPad mini, air, pro, etc.

Smart Keyboards

You can get USB and bluetooth keyboard from a variety of different manufacturers, not just Apple, and make a great little alternative to the on screen keyboard, when you are doing a lot of typing, writing or emailing.

Cases

A case is a must. You can get hundreds of different types. The ones I find most useful are ones that allow you to stand your iPad up making it great for watching movies. The case folds over covering the screen of the iPad when not in use.

USB Adapters

These come in useful when you want to connect something to your iPad that doesn't use USB-C. Devices such as keyboards, mice, external hard drives, USB memory sticks, cameras, some models of printers and memory card readers.

AV Adapters

AV Adapters are useful if you want to connect your iPad to a TV, Monitor or Projector.

You can buy a small USB C adapter that plugs into the port on the bottom of your iPad and will enable you to connect to an HDMI or DVI/VGA connector on your TV or Projector. Most modern TVs and Projectors are HDMI.

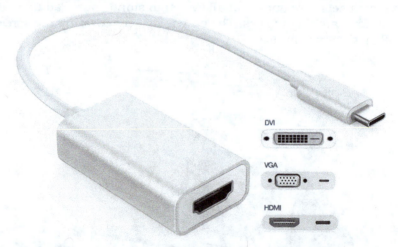

Get the adapter that has the correct video port on the other side, depending on what you're planning to connect.

Power Chargers

You can get a whole range of chargers from all different manufacturers. The most useful ones I have found are the ones that have a powered USB port on the side, that allows you to plug in your iPad and any other tablet for that matter, using the cable that came with it.

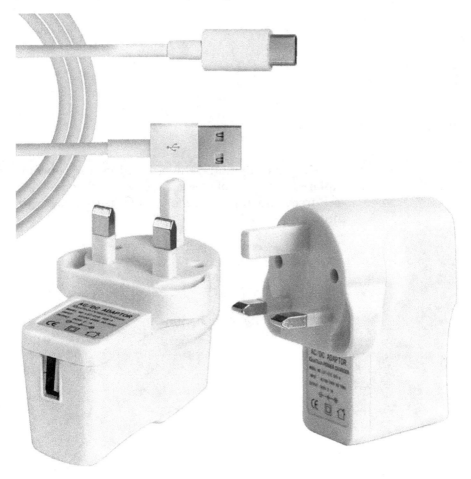

Your iPad will come with a charger so you won't need to buy one unless you need a replacement.

Video Resources

To help you understand the procedures and concepts explored in this book, we have developed some video resources and app demos for you to use, as you work through the book.

To find the resources, open your web browser and navigate to the following website

www.elluminetpress.com/resources/ipad-pro

At the beginning of each chapter, you'll find a website that contains the resources for that chapter.

When you open the link to the video resources, you'll see a thumbnail list at the bottom.

Click on the thumbnail for the particular video you want to watch. Most videos are between 30 and 60 seconds outlining the procedure, others are a bit longer.

When the video is playing, hover your mouse over the video and you'll see some controls...

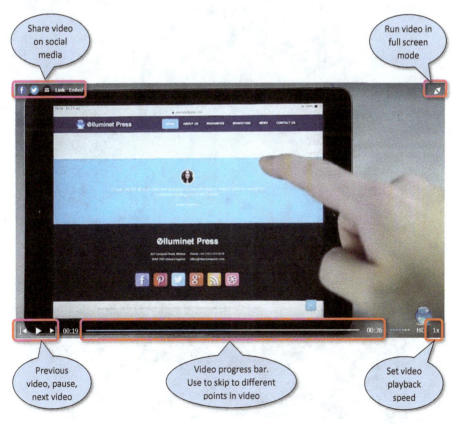

Appendix A: Video Resources

Throughout the book you'll come across QR codes and web links. These provide a quick access link to the videos.

You'll be able to scan the QR code or enter the link into your web browser. To scan the QR code, you'll need a QR code scanner.

If you're using an iPhone or iPad, simply open the camera app, point it at the code, and tap the link that appears to open it up. This will take you to the video demo on the website.

If you are using an Android device, you'll need to download a QR Code Scanner from the Google Play Store. To do this, open Google Play Store on your device and search for QR Code Reader. Tap QR Code Reader in the list, then tap 'install'.

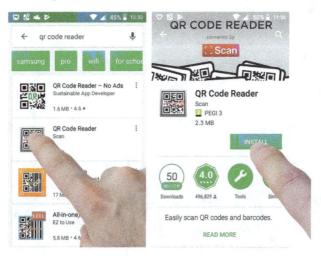

Open the QR Code Reader App, point the camera at the QR Code, then tap OK to open the link.

Index

Index

Index

T

Index

U

V

W